Sharp Women is a timely and thought-provoking read, filled with great advice on safety, security, and the importance of situational awareness.

Fred Burton, former US Diplomatic Security Service special agent and *New York Times* best-selling author

Kelly Sayre is just like you, or my sister, or my wife. But there is a notable difference. She decided to take ownership over her personal safety and began a journey investigating the world of personal security for women. Life is full of risk; there is no way to perfectly safeguard your life. But you can learn to make yourself a much less attractive target by being responsible for your own security. This outstanding book distills Kelly's findings into simple, easy-to-follow tips and tools. It is an invaluable resource for women who want to take ownership of their personal security and, in doing so, perhaps become more empowered in other areas of life. Written by a female for other females, it fills a needed place in the security market. You will be safer if you apply what she shares.

Doug Patteson, CFO, Turbocam Inc., former CIA officer, SPYEX and security/intelligence consultant

As a female and a security professional, I was thrilled to read Kelly's new book and discover someone who actually gets it when it comes to violence prevention. She understands the proactive thought process and real situational tactics that will keep you safe. A must-read for women who desire to take action and enhance their personal safety!

Denida Zinxhiria Grow, Founder of Athena Worldwide and Nannyguards, Protective and Intelligence Services

Two critical components that significantly contribute to one's safety are the gift of intuition and situational awareness. Kelly Sayre provides the reader with guidance and great examples of what to do in advance of a compromising or dangerous situation. After reading Kelly's book, readers will have a plan of action to go to in a time of compromise or conflict.

Steve Kardian, author of *The New Superpower for Women*, media personality, and safety expert

Sharp Women is a solidly grounded guide to women's personal protection. Kelly's insightful perspective empowers readers with effective and proactive principles to put to use immediately. I highly recommend it.

Boris Milinkovich, CD, CBCP, author of *The True North Tradecraft Disaster Preparedness Guide*, and CEO/Training Director of True North Tradecraft

SHARP
WOMEN

**Embrace Your Intuition,
Build Your Situational Awareness,
and Live Life Unafraid**

SHARP
WOMEN

**Embrace Your Intuition,
Build Your Situational Awareness,
and Live Life Unafraid**

K E L L Y   S A Y R E

Niche Pressworks

Sharp Women: Embrace Your Intuition, Build Your Situational Awareness, and Live Life Unafraid

ISBN-13:   978-1-952654-44-2 eBook
            978-1-952654-42-8 Hardback
            978-1-952654-43-5 Paperback

Library of Congress Control Number: 2021921771

Published by Niche Pressworks; http://NichePressworks.com
Indianapolis, IN

Dedication

For William and Alexander.
Your curiosity about the world helps me discover what I've missed.
Your boldness in everything you do reminds me to be brave.
Your kindness for others gives me hope for the future.

I love you.

Acknowledgments

This is the hardest part of the book to write. How do I begin to thank everyone who crossed my path and helped me get to this point without forgetting anyone? Every experience, good and bad, has made me who I am today. Every person I've crossed paths with has influenced me in some way. Perspective is everything.

I'm thankful for my faith. I know God is always with me, guiding me with a wicked sense of humor.

Marty—my partner in crime. Two stubborn, passionate, and bold alphas with intense senses of humor should probably never get married, let alone create two tiny humans who get a double dose of those characteristics. But I didn't get the memo; did you? We've been writing our own story since day one, and I look forward to all the chapters ahead. I love you and the family we created.

My family—Dad, Mom, Nick, Amanda, Becky, Josh, and all my extended family members. Thank you for the lessons, laughs, and love.

My California family of choice—after one of the most painful times in my life, you helped me find my inner spark again.

Sar/LL/Thelma—I could write a book solely about our adventures over the decades, but I'm not sure the statute of limitations is up. You have shown me what unconditional love for another human is all about. I'm so glad you asked to borrow a pencil at placement testing.

LJ—thank you for teaching me that a high-heel shoe is a viable weapon. You are one of the most resilient and "no BS" people I know. I raise a glass of Benedetto's wine to you, and I look forward to making many, many more memories.

Sarah—thank you for not ghosting me after I spilled my guts on our first "date." I'm grateful for MP because we would never have enough time to catch up otherwise. I promise to always have hummus and chips on hand.

Erin—your investigative and urban surveillance skills are better than any acronym agent in the world. You have a heart of gold and work harder than anyone I know. You are the epitome of "keep your eyes on the quiet ones; they get it done."

Morgan, Kathryn, Rosie, Rach, Melonie, Marcy, Kerry, Shelly, Anne, Greta, Kinko, Jenn, Haleigh, Nikki, Chelsea, Lindsay, Sofia, Deb, Melissa, Lorraine, Nik, Jackie, Renee, Jordan, and any other IG sisters I might have missed—I hope to meet all of you in person someday. The drive I witness in every one of you inspires me every day.

Ben, Boris, TJ, Echo, Drew, Doug, Josh, Fred, Ed, Jacques, Sean, John, Jim, Andy, Sonny, Mike, Chris, Robbie, Phillip, Gary, Marcus, Adam, Chris, Chase, Steve, Matthew, Brian, Jeffrey and any other IG brothers I might have missed—each of you has taken the time to answer my questions, promote my work, checked in on me, and given me shit as only a brother can. Thank you.

Thank you, Kasey, Tammy, Randy, Rory, and the VioDy OGs I've had the opportunity to play with—I've never had more fun learning how not to get my butt kicked … by getting my butt kicked. Sincerely, Starbuck.

Tammy, Kasey, M.E., Liisa, Ali, Tia, Cynthia, Lisa, Sheena, Mary, Heidi, Amy, Mimi, Sydney, Taylor, Deb, Mackenzie, Ryan, Rory, Ben, and Bob, the virtual 500rising crew—the tide is rising. Thank you for being awesome humans. I'm fortunate to stand shoulder to shoulder with you to change the discussion around violence against women.

To Bill, Steve, Gabrielle, Lynn, Carrie, Randy, Jameson, Shelley, Sarah-Marie, and all the other women and men in the personal protection/self-defense/threat assessment space I've connected with—thank you for spending time with me and sharing your knowledge. I was a complete stranger seeking to gain knowledge; the minutes and hours you spent sharing your insights with me are invaluable.

Thank you to the many awesome women and men who have championed me and my work over the years. The references, referrals, leads, and promotion of my work have humbled me.

Vicki and Nicole—I feel like I've known you both my whole life. Thanks for introducing us, Greg.

Thanks to the No Name HH crew. We had the best intentions of being a book club, but instead, it turned out to be a business idea incubator. Special shoutout to Sara—when I voiced doubts about teaching situational awareness as a business idea, you blurted out, "Aren't you worried if you don't do this, women will die?!?" We all laughed at your bluntness, but it was the kick in the pants I needed.

Nicole, Kim, and the other awesome people behind the scenes at Niche Pressworks—no one would be reading this book if it wasn't for all of you getting me through the process. Thank you! It has been a long and wonderful journey.

To Kent—thank you for keeping me legal and working to find the business strategy for DAG. Your belief in me and my work has gotten me through moments of doubt.

To Kami—you whipped me into the best shape of my life and helped me fall in love with weightlifting. Beyond building my physical strength and self-confidence, your friendship built my mental strength to get through the hard times.

To "Daria"—your strength and resilience are inspiring. I know your journey is not done. I look forward to cheering you on, every step of the way.

There are so many more people I am grateful to have crossed paths with along my life's journey. To any whom I have forgotten to mention, please accept my sincerest apologies.

Table of Contents

Trigger Warning

The opening chapter of this book contains a transcript from a domestic violence event recording. It contains swearing, threats of violence, and general subject matter that may upset some readers. In addition, other parts of the book discuss general situations and types of threats that may trigger emotional sensitivities.

This book is meant to help those in difficult situations, not to cause additional suffering. In the interest of preserving your mental health as well as your physical safety, please proceed at your own emotional pace, and seek assistance from a licensed mental health therapist if needed.

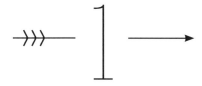

Daria's Story

You can recognize survivors of abuse by their courage.
When silence is so very inviting, they step forward and
share their truth so others know they aren't alone.

—Jeanne McElvaney

*M*itchell: *"Somebody come here, so I can punch them in the fucking head."*

Daria: *"If you want to fight, go to the bar."*

Mitchell: *"No, I want one of you fuckers."*

Daria: *"We are not going to fight you. You need to calm down."*

(12-year-old son screams in the background)

Daria: *"Mitchell! Mitchell! Get the fuck off of him."*

Mitchell: *"I never touched him."*

Daria: *(telling her son and daughter) "Go to Nana's and call 911."*

Mitchell: *"I never touched him."*

The Fairytale Beginning

Daria grew up a headstrong and independent young woman. Her family was one of prominence in her small town. Her dad owned the bus company that transported the local kids to and from school. Being the baby of the family, she was accustomed to using her voice to get attention. Daria's rebellious streak and low-key smarts kept her in the middle of her classmates socially, and she easily floated between the "who's who" and the "too cool for school" crowds.

At the age of nineteen, she became pregnant and welcomed a beautiful baby girl nine months later. Her Christian parents were not thrilled about her having a child out of wedlock, and she felt pressured to marry the father of her daughter. Daria liked him, but she wasn't in love with him. While in the process of purchasing their first home after the wedding, she discovered her new husband was having an affair. Infidelity was an acceptable reason for divorce in her Christian community, and as the primary breadwinner, she could purchase the home on her own for her and her daughter.

Being a single mom didn't diminish her career ambitions, and she bought the bus company from her dad. Her moxie showed at school board meetings as she negotiated transportation contracts with people twice her age. They wanted to dismiss her as someone who had been handed a company from Daddy, not a woman who made her own way. Daria worked hard to prove to the community that she had business smarts and the work ethic to follow through with her commitments. She emerged from her dad's shadow and gained a reputation as a respected business leader.

Attending a local wedding with friends and her soon-to-be-divorced sister Denise, Daria crossed paths with Mitchell for the first time. But it was Denise to whom Mitchell was first attracted. Denise's ex-husband had been abusive, and Mitchell saw her vulnerability as something he could manipulate in private. Unaware of Mitchell's dark secrets, Daria and her friends played matchmakers and encouraged Denise to go out with the charming wedding guest. Six weeks later, Mitchell broke things off with Denise by leaving a message on her answering machine. He then began focusing his attention on Daria.

He was the hometown hero cop, and she was the savvy female business owner juggling the duties of motherhood on her own. Mitchell's over-the-top affection and attention were something Daria craved but didn't want to admit she wanted. After years of managing all the details of a small business and a growing toddler on her own, it felt good to have someone who was willing to step up and take charge. The first family holiday gathering was a bit awkward since Mitchell was now dating Daria and not her sister. Secretly Daria thought, "My sister missed out!"

One year later, Mitchell and Daria were engaged. He was sweet, caring, and compassionate with Daria and treated her daughter as his own kid. Unlike most grooms-to-be, who are hands-off when it comes to wedding planning and just want to know what to wear and when to show up at the church, Mitchell had a different approach. He wanted to be involved in all the decision-making, right down to picking out bridesmaid dresses and deciding who would be invited to Daria's bachelorette party. By the time the wedding was three months away, Mitchell had taken over all the planning.

When Daria tried to give input or offered to help, Mitchell turned her down. His reason? He was naturally detail oriented and loved to plan parties and celebrations. He had everything under control so Daria could relax and focus on being a princess on their wedding day. Since her first marriage was under less-than-ideal circumstances, part of her enjoyed Mitchell taking charge of the planning. Her friends and family members commented about what a wonderful and caring husband he was going to be, judging by how he had taken on all the wedding responsibilities and tasks so Daria could enjoy the wedding day. She was a lucky woman!

But a voice in her head said something was off. When Daria suggested she and her best friend help with even a little bit of the planning, Mitchell said no. After all, as he liked to remind her, it was his first wedding and her second.

The First Alarm

Daria tried to enjoy her lack of wedding planning responsibilities, but her take-charge nature couldn't sit still. She found herself getting into small arguments with Mitchell over and over again. The moxie that helped her win tough contract negotiations with condescending school board members was not content with someone else making all the decisions. In the middle of yet another heated argument at his house, Daria told Mitchell the wedding was off and went to remove her engagement ring. But it was stuck on her finger.

If this were the script of a rom-com Hollywood movie, this would be the perfect comedic break. The frustrated fiancé would realize he's gone overboard and drop a sarcastic one-liner: "Well, it looks like you're stuck with me," and the stubborn bride-to-be would stifle a laugh and glare at him with a sassy pout. "This is not funny!" At this point, both they and the audience would laugh. The stress of the argument would dissolve, the couple would make a compromise, and the pre-wedding bliss would return.

But Hollywood is not real life.

Because she was fired up and angry, Daria couldn't get the ring off, no matter how hard she tried. Exasperated, she said, "I'll bring the ring back tomorrow. I'm leaving now!" Mitchell moved to block the door and told her in a cold voice that sent a shiver down her spine, "You're not leaving with my ring."

She had never seen this behavior or heard this tone from him in the past.

As Daria went to push past him and out the door, he shoved her back. Shocked by his aggressive response, she called him out, "You just pushed me! You put your hands on me!"

Immediately Mitchell's demeanor switched, and he started apologizing, "I didn't mean to! I just love you so much, and I can't have you leave. I'm so sorry!" Still in shock but no less angry, Daria repeated, "I'm leaving, and I'll put the ring in the mailbox tomorrow." She told him he wouldn't even need to see her.

As Daria made another attempt to get past Mitchell and out the door, he grabbed her left wrist, brought her hand up, and tried to remove the ring himself. She screamed at him to stop, telling him he was hurting her.

Mitchell got inches away from her face. With gritted teeth, he told her, "I will fucking break your finger; get that God-damn ring off now." A sense of fear washed over her. As her body's natural survival response drained the blood from her extremities, she was able to get the ring off. Daria ran out the door of his house and to her car. She drove home and broke down in tears.

The next day, Mitchell showed up at her front door with flowers. He apologized profusely for his actions the night before. He swore it had never happened before and would never happen again. He told Daria he had already called a therapist and made an appointment to get himself help. He said he had been more scared than her during their fight.

Daria took him back. A few weeks later, they were married.

Mitchell's "never happen again" promise only lasted until the honeymoon.

Behind Closed Doors

Everyone saw Daria and Mitchell as the power couple in town. He was the hero cop, working to keep crime out of their community.

She was the bus company owner, providing safe transportation for kids attending school. Mitchell was proud to fill the role of dad for Daria's daughter. After the couple exchanged vows on their wedding day, he turned to her daughter, got on one knee, and presented her with a necklace. He promised they would be a family.

Since Daria and Mitchell had their own homes before the wedding, they decided to list them both for sale. When one home sold first, they would pull the other one from the market and live in it. Daria got an offer on her house, and the sale was made final. They would be calling Mitchell's house home. Daria didn't know Mitchell had gotten three offers on his house, and he had turned them all down. He never intended to move into her house.

From the beginning, they were always working on their relationship. It was never "good." Every time Daria thought they were close to figuring things out between them, Mitchell would change the standards.

"Once we get married, things will be better."

"Once we sell one house and move in together, things will be better."

"Once we have a child together, things will be better."

"Once we make it past our five-year anniversary [because Mitchell said most law enforcement marriages fail within five years], things will be better."

"Once we have a second child together, things will be better."

In the early years, the voice in Daria's head would tell her, *You and Mitchell are the power couple in town; you can't divorce him. Think of what that would do to your credibility as a business owner! No one will believe you.* Outside the four walls of their home, Mitchell was the hometown cop, the little league coach, the caring, loving role model for all kids. Daria learned early in their marriage that if she did not support that façade in public, she would pay for it at home. She was forced to lie about his behaviors to her family and friends. No one knew what was really going on behind closed doors. After years of Daria publicly praising Mitchell, who would believe stories about the monster he became in private?

His House, His Rules

In his house, Daria and the kids were not allowed to use Mitchell's things. *His* stuff was *his* stuff. They were not allowed to sit in *his* chair or place anything on *his* desk. She was not allowed to use the washer, dryer, or dishwasher because *he* paid for them. He told her over and over again that she was dumb. That she would break *his* appliances if she used them. Daria was not allowed to park in *his* garage. She was not allowed to change the temperature on *his* thermostat. Daria could use *his* TV when he wasn't home, but he forbade her from using *his* DVD player, game systems, or anything else attached to *his* TV. She didn't even dare think of touching *his* computer.

Daria and the kids were isolated from friends and family. The kids were not allowed to go to friends' houses. They were not allowed to have friends overnight or even over to play. Mitchell made an exception one time and allowed each kid to have a few friends over for a birthday party, but only the kids he coached in sports or Cub Scouts could be invited. Daria's mom could only come over when she called first and he said it was okay, even though she lived just across the street. Most times, he didn't allow Daria's mom in the house. Daria wasn't allowed to go anywhere without his permission, and while she was gone, he would text or call constantly. She usually ended up leaving early because of his harassment.

Many times, Mitchell said he was going to kick Daria and the kids out of the house until they could learn to behave by his rules. During many of their late-night fights, Daria threatened to take the kids and leave him. Mitchell merely responded by waking up the kids and making them put stuff in a bag. Right before they walked out the door, he inevitably stopped the kids and told Daria she wasn't taking them away from him. She could leave, but the kids were staying. Daria would not leave her kids, and he knew it.

Daria asked multiple times for a divorce. She asked to handle it amicably, like adults. She would split custody with him and not ask for child support or alimony, and they could live separate, happier lives. Mitchell repeatedly refused, telling her he would get divorced *"over your dead body."*

She knew he wasn't kidding because she had seen how his mind worked. She had watched him quietly wait years to seek revenge on unsuspecting family members who had made him angry. He had told her many times that she would not take his children. He had explained how, if she left him and tried to hide, he would use his friends and family to find her. He had also explained in great detail how he could get away with her murder—how he could beat the legal system, how he could lie in court and falsify evidence. He had clearly illustrated that she would get nothing if she filed for divorce—if she lived long enough, that was. In Daria's mind, ***if she tried to leave Mitchell, she would be dead.***

(Scene continued from the beginning of the chapter)
Mitchell: "You better run and get her (their daughter). I never touched him (their son)."
Daria: "Get away from me."
Mitchell: "Keep walking, and we get closer to my gun."
Daria: "Get away from me."
Mitchell: "Keep walking. We'll get closer to my gun."
Daria: "I'm trying to get away from you. Stop it. You need to calm down."
Mitchell: "I will. If I'm going to jail, I'm gonna earn it."
Daria: "I can't stop it. It's too late." (referring to telling their daughter to go to Nana's and call 911)
(In the audio, you can hear the sound of Mitchell's gun safe opening.)

Daria: "Oh my God. Stop!"
Mitchell: "I'm tired of being pushed—"
Daria: "Put your gun away."
Mitchell: "Nope. And if I'm going to jail—"
Daria: "I can't stop it!"
Mitchell: "Like I said, if I'm going to jail, I'm going to earn it."
Daria: "Get your gun away from me. Get your gun away from me!"
*Mitchell: "Cops come knockin' on my door, you're dead. All they gotta
    do is come bangin' on the door and boom, boom."*
Daria: (sobbing) "I don't want to die!"
*Mitchell: "Then, make the phone call. You started this shit. You will
    end it. One way or the other."*
Daria: "I don't want to die! Please put the gun away!"

Mitchell threatened Daria with his gun to her head for almost
five more minutes. When the cops showed up, he miraculously put
his gun back in the safe and calmly walked outside to talk to the
chief of police, his boss. Daria left their house and crossed the street
to her mom's house.

That was where a deputy approached her and attempted to get
her to tell him what had happened. She told him several times that
she didn't want to say anything because the last time she reported
Mitchell, nothing happened to him. The deputy persisted.

Daria had her cell phone with the recording of the fight in her
pocket, but she still didn't know if the deputy would believe it.
After years of watching Mitchell get away with everything he had
done to them, she felt powerless.

That was when the deputy said something that changed Daria's
life forever.

He told her that they both knew it only gets worse.

That the next time Daria and Mitchell got in a fight, it would
be worse.

Daria realized what that meant—*if she stayed with Mitchell, she'd be dead.*

She reached into her pocket, pulled out her cell phone, and played the recording for the deputy.

Forty-Eight Hours

During all the years Daria had secretly dreamt of leaving Mitchell, she had imagined he would be behind bars for months, giving her plenty of time to pack up belongings and find a safe place for her and their children to live. But the reality was that as a "first-time offender," Mitchell was released on bail in just over forty-eight hours.

Before the fateful fight, she had control over nothing and was not allowed to make any decisions. Now she found herself needing to make all the decisions and make them quickly. That reality in itself was overwhelming. Add on top of that, she had no source of income and couldn't stay with family or friends because that would be the first place Mitchell would look for her. Meanwhile, getting a court date would take months.

As she faced each day, struggling to overcome the trauma of the last fifteen years and make a new life for herself and her kids, she kept asking herself, "How did I let it get this far? What were the signs I missed? Why didn't I listen to my intuition way back then?"

What she didn't realize at the time was that she wasn't alone. Little girls are raised to be kind, to share, to be quiet, and to respect others. Somewhere along the journey to adulthood, when girls speak up or question when something doesn't feel right, others say things such as, "You're overreacting," "You're reading into it too much," "Don't be so emotional," or, "That's crazy; you are exaggerating what happened."

Society and the influential people in our lives tell women to disregard our intuition signals. Because no one else can see from our perspective, we start to doubt that inner voice telling us something is wrong.

It's easy for you and me to make assumptions about Daria's choices because we weren't there. Abusive relationships don't start with the horrible and graphic violence committed at the end; they start with subtle nuances and small damages to a woman's boundaries and self-confidence. Many of those damages come in the form of emotional abuse and controlling behaviors—people often dismiss such behaviors as charming, persistent, loving, and protective. This book offers a new perspective on recognizing how those with bad intentions can manipulate socially accepted behaviors. It will help you see the skills you already have and use every day in a new and empowering way.

You were born sharp. Cutting through the crap life has thrown at you didn't break you; it simply dulled your edge. It's time to sharpen your skills and take charge of your own safety.

The Real Enemy of Women

Today you are you, that is truer than true. There is no one alive that is you-er than you.

—Dr. Seuss

n every example described within a book about situational awareness for women, you might expect the main enemy to be a person. That's true from one perspective. Depending on which study you read, the person committing violence against a woman is 85-95 percent likely to be someone she knows. Only a small percentage of violent attacks against women come from complete strangers. If you are more likely to know your attacker, why is it so hard to recognize and respond to the signs of an attack before it happens?

I believe the answer is that your real enemy isn't a person. Instead, it's the social mores you believe and follow. Social mores are informal codes of behavior established by a social group. These codes are not binding like laws.[1] Social conventions are similar;

---

[1] N. Sam, M.S., "Social Mores," *PsychologyDictionary.org*, April 13, 2013, https://psychologydictionary.org/social-mores/.

they are the established rules, procedures, and methods accepted as a guide for proper social conduct. Etiquette and social decorum are examples of social conventions.[2] You unconsciously adopt these behaviors and assumptions through your life experiences and the influence certain people have had in your life. Unfortunately, these codes of behavior don't always make sense.

Who Are YOU?
Not Who the World Tells You to Be

Adults commonly ask kids, "What do you want to be when you grow up?" No matter what the kid says, most of the time, adults go along with it. You want to be an astronaut and bake cakes? Great! You want to be a teacher and build skyscrapers? Wonderful! You want to make movies and sell cars? That sounds like lots of fun!

As those kids start to get older, the adult's response to the answer changes slightly.

"That's great, but you can't do both—you'll have to pick one."

"That's not a real career; you need to go to college and get a degree first."

"You don't want to do that job; no one likes people who do that for a living!"

Or the responses are even worse.

"You're not smart enough to do that."

"You're a girl; that's a job for boys."

"You can't have a good family life and a successful career; you'll have to pick one or the other."

Those types of comments stick in your head and shape the way you view yourself and the world around you. In reality, those types

---

[2] N. Sam, M.S., "Social Conventions," *PsychologyDictionary.org*, April 13, 2013, https://psychologydictionary.org/social-conventions/.

of comments come from adults projecting their own fears onto your dreams.

Acceptable Behaviors

What about your behaviors as a child? Did adults ever tell you that you were too loud or too emotional or too [fill-in-the-blank]? Perhaps you grew up in a community that had strict expectations for you. Maybe your religious beliefs expected you to fill specific roles when you became an adult.

It's an interesting juxtaposition. Society expects parents to raise "good girls" yet doesn't clarify how. Parents pass down the social mores they were raised with, believing these are "right." Each generation then repeats the cycle, whether it actually makes sense or not. What's the definition of insanity? Doing the same thing over and over again, expecting a different result. The general statistics of violence against women have remained steady for decades. If we want to decrease those numbers, it's time to look at the problem from a different perspective.

Girls' self-confidence greatly diminishes during middle school. I'm not sure if that's the moment the adult responses change from supportive to projective, but I can't help but think back to my own childhood and see a correlation in the timing.

I shifted back and forth between going my own way and wanting to gain approval from the adults I loved and respected. It was not the smooth, swinging motion you would expect from a pendulum. It was more like a really bad carnival ride that makes you want to vomit. While learning about situational awareness, I discovered the fascinating ways in which a little girl's upbringing can directly impact her personal safety as a grown woman.

I'm not talking about whether you grew up with an adult who taught you about the different self-defense tools or enrolled you in martial-arts classes. I'm talking about your mental well-being. I'm talking about your boundaries. I'm talking about your self-confidence.

'When I Grow Up'

What did you want to be when you grew up? When did that change for you? If you look around, you'll notice many "experts" who want to sell you the secret to finding you. However, I believe you already know you; you just packed that truth away to appease the outside world.

As the oldest child in my family, I had a lot of responsibilities growing up. My dad, a truck driver, was gone during the week. I was expected to take care of my siblings and help around the house. I learned many great life lessons growing up that way. However, the other side of that coin was that I never really thought about what I wanted. I always focused on what others needed me to do or be.

The things in life that make you feel fear are your social mores clashing with new information being received from your environment.

As an adult, when you're struggling to figure out who you are or what your strengths are, self-help books tell you to ask those around you for the answers. Instead, why not turn inwards and ask yourself who you are? Meditate on the questions or challenges you face to see what answers lie within you. Then, test those ideas through play or by experimenting with your thoughts. You may agree that you should "be true to yourself," no matter what anyone else thinks. But when the person telling you you're wrong is your mother, father, best friend, partner, or some other influential person in your life, things get twisted. Doubts creep in. You begin to second-guess yourself.

> *The things in life that make you feel fear are your social mores clashing with new information being received from your environment.*

When relationship counselors talk about how to get out of toxic relationships or how to prevent attracting toxic people, they always go back to the source of the problem: the lack of self-love. If you hear yourself saying, "This always happens to me," then you need to take a hard look at yourself and your behaviors. It's not easy—in fact, it's one of the most painful things to do. However, it's worth doing.

Your own behavior is 100 percent in your control, and being aware of what you're doing puts you in a much better situation. When you take responsibility for the things you control—your words, actions, boundaries—you take back your power and improve your self-confidence.

Outdated Social Mores

Women face potential threats starting at a very young age and often from inconspicuous sources. Society attempts to surround kids with those who are supposed to take care of and protect them from harm. Any threats to a child's safety can physically and psychologically affect that person throughout their lifetime. Unfortunately, a young child's limited verbal articulation skills might cause an adult to minimize the child's perceived threat. The adult might tell the child they're overreacting or being dramatic. When a trusted and influential adult insists a child's perspective is wrong, this breaks down the child's trust in their own intuition signals.

For example, adults probably cautioned, "Don't talk to strangers," when you were growing up. However, attacks by strangers make up only 21 percent of violent crimes—the rest are from someone known to the victim.[3]

---

[3] "Crime Data Explorer," Federal Bureau of Investigation, accessed October 27, 2021, https://crime-data-explorer.app.cloud.gov/pages/explorer/crime/crime-trend.

The other problem with this statement goes back to the concern of giving a vague or confusing message. The word "stranger" can be confusing for kids.

When you tell kids, "Don't talk to strangers!" but then force them to do so in certain situations, you send a mixed message. For instance, you might compel your child to say "hi" to new people at community social functions or greet unfamiliar relatives at family gatherings. Yet, these people are technically strangers to the child. Also, the idea of not talking to strangers doesn't make practical sense. Part of growing up involves expanding our social network and meeting new people. Therefore, kids have to get comfortable with talking to strangers as they grow up.

Here's another example of mixed messages. Young children are told, "No one has permission to touch you when you don't want to be touched," and yet in the next breath, "Give Grandma a hug because she wants one."

Or, how about this dilemma? "If a stranger asks for help finding their lost puppy, say no!" Yet, "Always be kind, polite, and helpful to others."

One of my favorites people told me when I was a young girl was, "Never go anywhere alone." Yet, society makes fun of women for going to the bathroom in groups.

Yes, dangerous strangers exist in the world, but it's similar to the assumption discussion from earlier. When you use broad terms and unclear guidance, kids make assumptions about what you mean based on their life experiences. The more hypocrisy they experience ("Don't talk to strangers but say hello to my co-worker you've never met before"), the more kids question their intuition signals.

I'm sure you can think of other examples of mixed messages you've heard and probably repeated to kids. Don't beat yourself up! You were operating under the assumption that everyone knows how to apply the rules in the appropriate context. From one generation to the next, these assumptions are based on and become what is sometimes called "social contracts."

A social contract is "an actual or hypothetical agreement among the members of an organized society or between a community and its ruler that defines and limits the rights and duties of each."[4] A person carries these social contracts forward at each new stage of life, often without adapting the parameters to match the new environment.

Think back to when you were growing up, and let's use the "don't talk to strangers" example. I'm guessing you went from day-care or home life to a school system of some sort. As you advanced through the different stages of life, you encountered new people (strangers) telling you how to behave and establishing rules you needed to follow. You probably thought, "Wait, I'm not supposed to talk to strangers, but these strangers are okay?"

After eighteen years of navigating the social contracts surrounding you, you were ready to step out on your own, spread your wings, and fly. Those social contracts were now deeply ingrained in your subconscious. They became the shortcuts your brain took to help you make decisions. Even if the social contracts didn't apply to your circumstances anymore, you still filtered all your sensory inputs through those filters. Another term associated with this is "unconscious (or implicit) bias."

Unconscious bias (also known as implicit bias) is a learned assumption, belief, or attitude that exists in the subconscious.[5]

A good example of unconscious bias is the cultural aspect of "personal space." In Argentina, it's normal to stand close—within a mere 2.5 feet of strangers when talking to them. However, in Romania, the social contract or expected distance is 4.5 feet when

---

[4] "Social contract," Merriam-Webster Online Dictionary, accessed October 27, 2021, https://www.merriam-webster.com/dictionary/social%20contract.

[5] "19 Unconscious Biases to Overcome and Help Promote Inclusivity," Team Asana, May 27, 2021, https://asana.com/resources/unconscious-bias-examples.

talking to people you don't know.[6] So if you're a Romanian exchange student studying in Argentina, you may think Argentinians are rude because they get so close during your conversations with them. But an Argentinian in Romania might think the Romanians were rude or strange for giving so much space to strangers.

How does unconscious bias impact your personal safety? Think about this: these vague ideas of when and how you could be "in danger" do not help you. They are based on ominous general descriptions and labels that don't help you identify specific threats in actual reality. They also don't give you any practical information about handling them. If you haven't learned how to read and react to strange behaviors from others, set and enforce your boundaries, and make your personal safety a priority, you have probably faced some challenges in protecting yourself—even as an adult.

Frankly, learning to adult is exhausting. You try so hard to do the right thing. But "right" is vague and subjective as passed down from an authority figure, and it is based on social contracts that might no longer apply to your environment. Sometimes, misinterpretation of the result of the ill-fitting, unclear guidelines can cause temporary embarrassment. For instance, my sixteen-year-old self blurted out, "Well, at least I'm not an a**hole like you," after a demeaning boss remarked, "I would never want to be a lowly busser like you." (Yes, it's good to speak up for yourself, but maybe try not to swear in front of customers.) Unfortunately, sometimes, there's a much more tragic outcome.

What are your beliefs about yourself regarding your personal safety? Would you be able to tell a stranger sitting too close to you to move over? What if the person in your personal space is someone

---

[6] Melanie Radzicki McManus, "Which Countries Have the Smallest Personal Space?" HowStuffWorks, accessed October 27, 2021, https://science.how stuffworks.com/life/inside-the-mind/human-brain/which-countries-have -smallest-personal-space.htm.

you know? If it were your boss, a co-worker, an acquaintance, or someone you're in a relationship with, could you still tell them to move over with conviction? What if that person has predatory behaviors? For instance, what if the boss starts rubbing the back of your neck, or the friend of a friend goes in for a second hug because he says you didn't hug him enough the first time? What if your male friend makes fun of your boundaries? Do you feel you can say something?

If you're thinking, "Of course I would say something! That's completely inappropriate!" that's great. That's the mindset you need to have, AND you need to dig into that a little more deeply.

However, if those who raised you placed social mores upon you to follow the rules, not be loud, respect others, and be kind, but never discussed when it was okay to break those rules, those guidelines will impact your interactions with others as an adult.

> *"The beliefs that influence us most in adult life were formed when we were kids."*
> —Tim Shurr

Self-Awareness Is Crucial

Have you taken one of the many personality surveys out there to find out who you are? It's like they hold some secret about you that you haven't discovered. A group of questions with a limited number of answers to pick from will tell you all you need to know about yourself.

Isn't that a bit ridiculous?!

I'm not saying these surveys are worthless; let me clarify. They are great tools that can help assess certain personality characteristics. Taking those assessments and making adjustments to your work and home lives to improve efficiency and quality is wonderful. But they are just tools. You can spend lots of money to have lots of tools in your toolbox. You can pay for the best of the best tools. But you can only use each tool for certain things, and tools can't fix things on their own. You have to pick them up and use them correctly.

This brings us back to square one—you. When was the last time you gave yourself space to meditate/reflect/process who you are? In this culture of hiring life coaches, taking personality surveys, and asking five people closest to you who you are, you've lost a very important and crucial voice—your own. Again, I'm not saying that asking for outside input is wrong, but you need to take the time to listen to your own voice. Only it can tell you what you like and don't like, what you're comfortable with and not comfortable with, and how you want to live your life.

An example of getting caught up in what others tell you about yourself comes from the movie *Runaway Bride* with Julia Roberts. In each of her relationships, she becomes a chameleon and adopts the same hobbies, tastes, and roles as her soon-to-be-left-at-the-altar fiancés. Only when Richard Gere's character points out her changing egg preference with each beau does she realize she has no idea how she likes her eggs cooked. Then there's a scene showing her in a kitchen with every different kind of egg dish you can imagine. Julia's character samples each one, and at the end of the movie, she proclaims her favorite—eggs Benedict.

I use this movie example because the scenario often plays out the same way in real life for women. Think about your past relationships, whether with friends or intimate partners. Can you think of at least one time your preferences or hobbies came from someone in your circle? It's not necessarily a bad thing! By trying something new with someone you know, you expand your world and have the opportunity to discover things you may never have tried on your own. However, I want you to take time to think about those things and make sure you actually like them.

Hollywood vs. Reality

Speaking of movies, Hollywood doesn't make blockbusters showing a woman living her best life without any threats to her personal safety. If she doesn't have some life-threatening situation to get through and overcome, the audience doesn't have any reason to get sucked in and watch until the end.

One staged self-defense video I watched depicts a woman in workout clothes who bikes past a stopped vehicle filled with four men. The driver's window is rolled down, and he reaches out to slap her butt as she rides by. Her response is to stop, get off her bike, and throw it against the car. There's no sound, but the woman and the driver are obviously exchanging heated words. He gets out, and she proceeds to get into a physical fight with him. The other guys get out of the car, and she takes on each of them in a physical fight until the guys are all down on the ground.

While the voice in my head was cheering for her, it's not a realistic scenario. First, she would potentially be seen as the aggressor and would face assault charges. But Hollywood rarely, if ever, talks about that angle.

Second, that mindset focuses on the physical fight aspect of self-defense, where it's all about how to respond with punches and kicks. However, from a more realistic self-defense training perspective, a much better response option would have been a Mace® spray attached to her hand while biking. Then, after the driver slapped her butt, she could decide whether to ignore him, say something, or simply stop, turn to the open window, and spray the occupants in the vehicle.

With the driver unable to see clearly enough to drive after her, she could bike away. The other occupants would also be coughing and very uncomfortable. I'm betting they wouldn't want to tell anyone about the incident. As an added bonus, I can't imagine what it would take to get Mace® out of a car's upholstery.

Let's Make 'Nothing' Sexy

In the hierarchy of personal safety, the highest order "win" is not being there in the first place.

> ### *Personal Safety Options*
> 1. Avoid.
> 2. Can't avoid? Leave.
> 3. Can't leave? De-escalate.
> 4. Can't de-escalate? Try leaving again.
> 5. If all of these fail, the solutions are physical.

But not getting in a physical fight doesn't make for good stories you share with friends.

"Hey friend, guess what? I walked from my car to work and then from work to my car without getting into a physical fight!"

As much as I would love to make avoidance the sexy thing to do, I'm not convinced society is ready for that. When nothing happens, no one can collect data points for statistics. No one feels compelled to tell stories about nothing happening.

I believe you have a story and history that made you who you are today. That history can either be in your way or strengthen you. This book will help you sharpen the skills you already have but may not know how to use. You will learn to embrace your intuition by understanding how the survival instinct process works. You will learn to take control of your situation by recognizing those wanting to manipulate you. You will learn to build your situational awareness and live life unafraid—as the Sharp Woman you were meant to be.

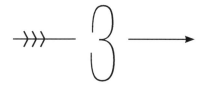

What Is 'Situational Awareness,' Anyway?

Having awareness means using your senses and intuition to notice something is "off" in your environment. Then, understanding what that means to you and your safety. Lastly, taking action to preserve your safety.

—Kelly Sayre

How does the domestic violence story at the beginning of this book relate to situational awareness? By being "situationally aware," you can quickly recognize behaviors that put your safety at risk. These behaviors could show up anywhere—at home, at work, or at places you go in your day-to-day life.

Fold in the Cheese

Before you learn how to be situationally aware, you have to understand what "situational awareness" actually means. Frankly, getting a decent definition for that can be challenging in itself. Personal safety instructors talk about situational awareness, but they often don't really define it—especially not from the female perspective. In fact, it reminds me of a particular segment from one of my favorite TV shows, *Schitt's Creek*.

In the scene, Moira and David, the mother and son lead characters, are attempting to cook enchiladas. It becomes very apparent that neither of them is comfortable in the kitchen; they have probably never cooked anything in their lives. With Moira reading from the recipe card, David is doing his best to follow her instructions.

"Next step is to fold in the cheese."

"What does that mean? What does 'fold in the cheese' mean?"

"You fold it in."

"I understand that, but how? How do you fold it? Do you fold it in half, like a piece of paper, and drop it in the pot, or what do you do?"

"David, I cannot show you everything."

"Okay, well, can you show me one thing?"

"You just …. Here's what you do. You just fold it in."

"Okay, I don't know how to fold broken cheese like that!"

"Then I don't know how to be any clearer!"

The more David asks for clarification, the more defensive and frustrated Moira becomes. She doesn't actually know what it means either, but she is not willing to admit it.

My personal "fold in the cheese" moment happened at the end of the first women's self-defense class I took. We had spent the four hours of class striking and kicking pads, running physical drills, and targeting. It was awesome, and I loved every minute of it.

As we sat down on the mats to stretch and cool down, the instructor stated something along the lines of, "Getting in a physical self-defense fight is the last thing you want to do. You need to be more situationally aware to avoid a fight in the first place. Goodbye!"

And then he sent us on our way.

My brain did a full stop with the instructor's last comment. But unfortunately, I was not like David in that moment. I did not blurt out, "What does being more situationally aware mean? What am I looking for? How will I recognize early signs of danger? How will I know if I'm paying attention to the right things? When I see danger, then what should I do?!"

I simply walked out of the class, dumbfounded.

I had just spent four hours learning physical skills I was supposed to *avoid* using if possible. The "thing" I was supposed to use 99.9 percent of the time wasn't discussed at all!

As I drove home, I started replaying the class in my head. I realized I had assumed self-defense was all physical skills, and I never considered the prevention side.

My Search for Answers

My curiosity went into overdrive. I needed to figure out what being "situationally aware" meant. I spent hours asking my husband, who has a military background and is in law enforcement, tons of questions. I searched the internet for training on the subject, only to find a few options geared to everyday people, but nothing specifically for women.

I didn't realize that simple comment at the end of class would be the start of a fascinating journey—a journey to gain the knowledge I now get to share with you in this book.

Limited Resources

During some of my initial research for information on situational awareness, I discovered Gavin de Becker's book, *Gift of Fear*.[7] I went to a local bookstore to purchase a copy in hopes of finding other

---

[7] Gavin de Becker, *Gift of Fear*, (New York: Dell Publishing, 1997).

books on the subject next to it on the shelf. When I didn't see any others, I asked a store associate if more books were located in another section. She searched their inventory, both in-store and online, and came up with nothing. So, I purchased Mr. de Becker's book and headed home.

I finished reading *Gift of Fear* in two days and was amazed at the knowledge and understanding I gained. The book was written in 1997. There had to be other resources on the topic by now!

It turned out, there was a lot of information and training on situational awareness skills, but it was geared toward law enforcement and military personnel. There wasn't a training program that translated those skills to women from the perspective of a woman.

The Missing Perspective

Law enforcement and military personnel go into many situations where their life is on the line. It is absolutely critical they learn how to recognize a threat, respond accordingly, and make a situation safe as quickly as possible.

But for women just living their daily lives, it's different. Women in these situations aren't necessarily aware when they are potentially in danger. After all, they are just going about their normal business—working, going out with friends, grocery shopping, or just hanging out at home. Most aren't deliberately going into recognized high-threat situations for a living.

When they become aware that someone may have ill intent, they have to manage that within their social relationships. Often, the person with ill intent has a more personal relationship with them than what happens in a typical military or law enforcement scenario—in fact, it's usually someone they know.

The more I asked self-defense or personal security instructors questions related to situational awareness—especially as it pertains to the everyday woman—the more I realized not a lot of people had thought about the specific issues women face. And then, I realized that part of the issue is that most self-defense instructors are male. As great as so many of them are at teaching physical defense and even pre-threat awareness, they have never been a woman. They don't have a full understanding of our viewpoint because they haven't lived our lives.

Don't get me wrong—I'm not at all bashing male instructors or even men in general. I firmly believe a rising tide lifts all ships, not just those piloted by female captains. My goal is not to criticize them or the industry but to help fill an information gap so anyone and everyone can learn how to keep themselves safer. My goal is to be a part of the conversation and provide an additional perspective.

You're Already a Sharp Woman

I'm willing to bet you instantly know when a friend is having a bad day. You know what a loved one is trying to say, even if they haven't said a word or your loved one is two years old and still learning to talk. You know when someone in your house is sneaking snacks based on the squeaking of the door hinges. You know that how you carry yourself as you walk across a room gives others a first impression of you. If you've ever driven a vehicle, you've already used an awareness skill called the "OODA Loop" (Observe, Orient, Decide, Act") to get from Point A to Point B. You just might not think about it or know the formal term for it.

The fact is, you were born a Sharp Woman. You've had to work hard to cut the crap out of your life, and that made your sharp skills a little dull. You're not broken; you only need sharpening. Steel sharpens steel. Strong women helping other strong women sharpens us all.

You use situational awareness skills every day. You've just never thought of them from the perspective of your personal safety. In my work, I really enjoy showing how these technical terms relate to every-day experiences or life skills and sharing my clients' "aha" moments.

Your Safety Is Your Responsibility

You cannot and should not rely on anyone else to keep you safe. Tony Blauer says, "Be your own bodyguard," and I agree with the sentiment.

But for me, the word "bodyguard" conjures up visions of a 6'4", 280 lb. muscle-bound dude with a scowl on his face in my head. That's not me, and I'm guessing that's not you, either.

So upon reading that, if you're like me, you might be thinking things like, "Be my own bodyguard! How? I don't have a back-ground in martial arts! I'm not law enforcement or military! I didn't grow up around firearms! I like to work out, but I can't out-muscle a predator! What do you mean I'm supposed to be my own body-guard? I already struggle to find time to do things I like to do. How am I supposed to find time to take classes and attend training sessions for years to increase my physical strength?!?"

But that's where situational awareness comes in. A bodyguard is someone who takes ownership of their client's safety—including being aware of potential threats before they happen.

You have the power to do that for yourself. You just need to learn some new ways to use your existing skills.

Do I believe we need to teach women physical self-defense? Yes. Plus, it's fun to get frustrations out by hitting pads. But do I think there's a huge opportunity to teach women how to avoid a physical altercation in the first place? Absolutely! To show you how these things work together, let's look at how I coached one of my clients.

Walking with Sue

Sue was a private coaching client who had come to me with con-cerns about a specific individual's threat to her personal safety.

Sue was already in discussions with law enforcement, her workplace, and family members about safety measures. She had plans in place in case the man tried to contact her or showed up at her work or home. She was having security lights and cameras installed at her home, and her workplace was implementing extra safety measures.

Some individuals recommended she carry a firearm, but she didn't own one and had no training. Since the individual would be released in a couple of weeks, she didn't have enough time to train properly. In addition, the nature of her job prevented her from carrying at all times.

Sue knew law enforcement was doing everything they could to be ready if he showed up at her door, but what about the time it took them to respond? What could she do in the critical one to three minutes before law enforcement arrived? What could she do if the man suddenly appeared in front of her as she went about her normal routine?

That's when a co-worker recommended she contact me.

I was able to walk alongside Sue, literally and figuratively, during our coaching session and point out ways she could keep herself safe during different situations. For instance, I taught her how to scan parked vehicles to see if anyone was watching her. I instructed her to do things such as pausing when she opened the heavy steel door as she left her office building, taking time to make sure he wasn't outside waiting for her. It was a secure entry point, so if she saw him, all she had to do was step back into the building and close the door. He would not be able to gain access, and she could get to safety.

We walked through her home and talked about what she and her husband could do if they thought he was trying to break in. I told her to think like Kevin from the *Home Alone* movies. We both laughed, but it was the truth! You want to make your home an attacker's worst nightmare.

I also helped prepare her for the event in which she would need to face a physical altercation. I brought every self-defense tool I carry so she could look at them, try them out, and decide what was best for her.

We talked through many mental plans to keep herself safe no matter how quickly law enforcement was able to respond.

This kind of thinking is not as difficult as you might fear. After almost every training session or presentation I give, someone responds, "What you said is common sense; I just never thought of it that way." That's my goal with this book. I hope you have lots of "aha moments" as you continue reading. And remember: I'm here to walk alongside you as a trusted guide. I'll hold the space for you to try new things, make mistakes, try again, and grow. I'll remind you that you never have to apologize about prioritizing your personal safety.

How Intuition Works

When I train my clients in situational awareness, one of the main things I focus on is using intuition.

Your intuition signals are your basic survival instincts trying to communicate with you. Women have unbelievable intuition skills. You know things without consciously knowing how you know things. Even at a young age, you could sense things about people and places. All of your senses are constantly taking in observations about your surroundings and the people in them. It's your sub-conscious' job to filter the information received from your senses and decide which information needs to get to your consciousness. This is a very important job! Can you imagine if you consciously observed every single thing your eyes saw, every sound your ears heard, every smell, every feeling, and every taste? It would be a sensory overload that would make the lights of Las Vegas seem dull. So how does your subconscious decide what to filter? The simple answer is that it uses the social mores established by your life experiences and the influence of the people around you.

It's like driving a car. If you've ever rear-ended a vehicle, your subconscious now has an intuitive filter for that. When one of your senses observes you getting too close to someone's rear bumper, your subconscious will tell your consciousness to hit the brakes. You don't want to wind up in an accident again! If you've never rear-ended a vehicle, your subconscious doesn't have a filter for that scenario, and your reaction time may be slower. I'm not suggesting that you don't have good defensive driving skills if you've never been in an accident. It's simply an example of an observation that trips your survival instinct and alerts your consciousness via an intuition signal.

Your subconscious works hard to filter the useful information you need to survive, but it doesn't have a lot of time to tell you exactly what observation tripped the intuition signal. It only needs you to take action immediately. The fancy term for the process is called "heuristics."

According to *Psychology Today*, a heuristic is "a mental shortcut that allows an individual to make a decision, pass judgment, or solve a problem quickly and with minimal mental effort."[8]

An everyday example of heuristics looks like this: Say you're going on a trip with a group. As you're rushing out the door, suddenly everyone has a million questions. "Where are we going?" "What are we doing?" "What time will we be back?" You respond with, "Once we're in the car and on the road, I can explain. Right now, I need everyone to get in the car so we can go!"

When your intuition signals that something is not right, especially concerning your personal safety, it doesn't have time to explain the details. It just needs you to take action.

---

[8] "Heuristics," *Psychology Today*, accessed October 27, 2021, https://www .psychologytoday.com/us/basics/heuristics.

It really is that simple. In *Gift of Fear*, de Becker reminds us that intuition is always right in at least two important ways:

1. It is always in response to something.
2. It always has your best interest at heart.[9]

Unfortunately, we humans screw it up by analyzing the intuition signal in the moment instead of trusting it. That's where self-doubt comes in.

Self-Doubt Is Your Enemy

One of the biggest problems with using intuition is a tendency to override it.

Has someone ever listened to a story about your intuition alarm bells going off and then told you that you were probably overreacting? They insist you were probably reading too much into it or that your emotions must have gotten the better of you.

Words matter. Especially when those dismissive comments come from someone you love and respect. It can cause you to start second-guessing your intuition, which means you internalize that voice and make questioning or doubting yourself a habit.

Maybe you were overreacting when you thought that man might be following you.

Maybe your friend's new boyfriend truly is a really friendly guy and loves giving long hugs to women, and your uneasiness is unfair to him.

That voice of doubt creeps into your head and plants itself firmly in your consciousness.

Unfortunately, the next time your intuition tries sending a signal to take action, that doubt puts up a yield sign.

"Whoa, whoa, whoa—are you overreacting again? Are you sure?" it asks.

---

[9] De Becker, *Gift of Fear*, 71.

Internally, your subconscious is trying to push through the intuition signal to your consciousness. It's screaming, "Yes, I'm sure! I can't explain right now, but you need to take action!" Externally, you look like a deer in headlights.

To make matters worse, if you did take action to get to safety when you felt an intuition signal, then you can't prove something would've happened had you not gotten safe. Remember what I said about "nothing" happening being its own problem regarding statistics? The same thing happens internally with you. The seed of doubt planted in your head by the person second-guessing your perspective now has no "proof" to show it's wrong. The more you water the seed of self-doubt with your lack of "proof," the more it grows, negatively impacting your self-confidence.

Unfortunately, this typically happens to young, school-aged girls. That confident little girl suddenly starts doubting herself.

This erosion of confidence can harm more than her general intuition. If she doubts herself too much, not only will she negate her own intuition, but she'll also attract predatory manipulators. As her self-confidence and self-worth decline, she will seek outside affirmation of her worth from those around her. If she seeks it from people who have ill intent, she will experience negative outcomes.

Your perspective is your reality. It's not right or wrong; it's your perspective. If you don't listen to and obey your intuition, you won't identify threats in time. It doesn't matter whether you were "right" or "wrong"; unfortunately, sometimes you can't prove that. You have to start celebrating "nothing" as the best outcome.

Have Realistic Expectations

The following chapters depict some typical women's personal safety situations and show ways to look at them differently.

However, before we move on, I need to set clear expectations so you know exactly what you'll get out of this book and what you won't.

First off, I will use the male pronouns to describe the predator because, in most instances, violence against women comes from a male. Yes, there are cases of women being the predator, and I acknowledge that. For the sake of this book, I'm focused on the early warning signs of potential violence, daily habits to sharpen your personal safety skills, and ways to build mental strategies for handling threatening situations.

Second, nothing in this book is guaranteed to work 100 percent of the time. There is no perfect answer or prescription for avoiding violence.

If you're wondering what you can do to prevent anything bad from ever happening to you or someone you love, I'm going to be honest with you—nothing. There is no such thing as perfect situational awareness. You cannot constantly be scanning your environment without making yourself look suspicious. Plus, sleep is important.

Women are more likely than men to be perfectionists, and I see this as one of the biggest challenges for women's safety training. Let go of thinking you have to have perfect awareness skills to stay safe. By practicing the daily habit exercises at the end of each chapter, you will vastly improve your situational awareness skills.

Sharp Women Pledge

It's time to make a commitment to your own personal safety. Put your name in the blanks of the pledge and get ready to show the world you are a Sharp Woman!

Take a picture of the pledge with your phone and make it your lock-screen image. You can even tear it out and hang it on your wall as a reminder. Whenever you see it, remember: YOU are a Sharp Woman who is getting sharper every day.

thediamondarrowgroup.com

Sharp Women Pledge

I, _____ , will never apologize for making my safety a priority.

My wants and needs matter. My perspective may be different than the next person's, but that doesn't make my view wrong. Using clear communication in a direct manner isn't being rude; it's honoring the boundaries I've set. I expect others to respect my mental, emotional, and physical boundaries. No one, not family, friends, colleagues, acquaintances, or even strangers, has the right to cross my boundaries.

I, _____ , am a Sharp Woman who will live life on my terms!

THE DIAMOND ARROW GROUP
An arrow through a diamond symbolizes courage moving forward.

Designed and letterpress printed at Bruno Press

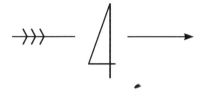

Am I Being Followed?

It's not about finding your voice, it's about giving yourself permission to use your voice.

—Kris Carr

Since I started The Diamond Arrow Group, all the women I've talked to have shared stories about intuiting that something wasn't right in their environment. I estimate that eight out of those ten stories involved thinking or knowing they were being followed.

Timing Is Key

Claudia is a bright, talented young woman who had the opportunity to live and work in London after high school. One evening after getting off the bus to walk the remaining few blocks home, she noticed a man had left the bus stop and started walking behind her. She caught his reflection in the shop windows as she walked. Realizing she was nearing the end of the shopping area and would be crossing a street to a quieter residential area, she decided to test her suspicions of being followed.

With doormen and shoppers filling the sidewalks, she had built-in witnesses and potential helpers if the man following her had ill intentions. She stopped, turned around to face the man, and loudly asked, "Are you following me?" Her bold question in a very public setting startled the man, and he immediately turned around and walked away.

Claudia used reflective surfaces (shop windows) to assess her situation. She remained aware, knowing when she would have fewer witnesses and helpers. She also remained confident, using her voice directly and clearly. All of these things made nothing happen. That is something to celebrate!

Well, what if he wasn't following her and was just walking the same direction, and she scared him with her abrupt question?

It doesn't matter.

Claudia never needs to apologize for making her safety a priority, and neither do you.

Maybe Claudia's situation doesn't seem to apply to you. Maybe you don't live in a large city. Maybe you've never ridden on public transportation because it's not available in your area. Here's another example most can relate to. Have you been to a shopping mall?

Trust Your Gut

Ann was a new mother with some free time one afternoon. She decided to get out of her house and head to the local mall. Getting the stroller out of the trunk, unfolded, and safely set up was still a bit of a challenge. There were so many mechanisms and latches to remember! Once the car seat was securely fastened, she made her way to the mall entrance.

She pushed the stroller into the first store and noticed a man in his fifties standing around. Her first thought was that the guy was probably shopping with his wife, and she continued looking at items.

In the next store, Ann recognized the same man from the first store. He was still just standing around, but no one resembling a wife or kids was in his proximity. Getting an intuition signal that something wasn't quite right with him, she left that store and made her way to the next.

While looking around the third store, she saw the man again. At this point, her intuition alarm signals were loud and clear, and she decided to leave the mall. Urgently pushing her stroller toward the car, she silently prayed that she would be able to secure her child in the backseat and wrangle the stroller into the trunk faster than ever before. She couldn't shake the chill creeping up her spine as she struggled with the cumbersome stroller. As she was shutting her trunk, she looked up and saw a man fast approaching.

It was the same man she had seen at each of the three stores, and he was headed directly toward her.

As her adrenaline spiked, she fumbled to get her keys out of her purse. As she reached for her driver's door, the man asked,

"Could you help me, or can I borrow your cell phone? My car isn't starting."

She replied with a straightforward "No," got in her car, locked her door, and drove away. Once Ann felt she was far enough away from the parking lot, she pulled over and called her dad. She was shaking from the adrenaline dump, and her words came out all jumbled. Hearing her dad's voice and realizing she was safe helped her calm down.

Once she was home and the stress of the moment was over, she was able to piece together what her senses had picked up that made her intuition alarm bells go off.

Breaking It Down Afterwards

Going back to the definition of heuristics that I shared, these were the points Ann realized later.

- ♦ The man was alone.
- ♦ He wasn't holding any shopping bags.
- ♦ He never made eye contact or crossed her path. He purposely avoided her, wanting to appear uninterested. In situations where you and another person keep ending up in the same location out of coincidence, there is a tendency to call it out and use comedy to break an uncomfortableness. You or the person may say, "I guess we have the same taste in shopping!"
- ♦ She left the third store and went straight to her car. How could he have left after her, gotten to his car, discovered something was wrong, and then found her amongst all the other vehicles in the parking lot?
- ♦ What fifty-something-year-old man is going to seek out a young mother to help with car problems? Why not go back into the mall to find security or the information desk?

As she shared the incident with her husband, all of these points came to her consciousness. In that moment of fumbling to get her keys as the man got closer, her subconscious didn't have time to break it down so pointedly. It simply sent an intuition signal—"get away now."

If she had ignored her intuition signal, we don't know what would've happened. Maybe nothing. But there is absolutely no reason for you or anyone else to feel obligated to stick around and find out. Remember, you never need to apologize for making your personal safety a priority.

Being Followed While Driving

A woman shared a story about her daughter being followed after she left a large retailer. As the daughter drove away from the parking lot and onto dark county roads, she noticed a car following her very closely. The car was flashing its lights, trying to get her attention and to get her to pull over. The daughter kept driving. Instead of going home, she drove to her fitness gym that had a key-card entry system. Later, she told her mom that she didn't want to lead them to her house, but she didn't want to call the cops because she wasn't 100 percent sure what was happening. The daughter didn't want to bother law enforcement if it was nothing.

I applaud the daughter's decision not to pull over or drive home. If the other driver does have ill intent, you do not want them to know where you live. Regarding not wanting to bother law enforcement, I will share the sentiment my husband always tells me. Law enforcement would rather take your call that turns out to be nothing than take a victim impact statement from you later. Even if you live in a remote area or law enforcement cannot respond right away, the dispatcher can collect important information.

In Claudia's, Ann's, and the daughter's stories, we will never know for sure what the outcome would have been if they had not prioritized their safety first.

So what happens if you get a spine-tingling intuition signal, take action, and it's a simple misunderstanding? What's the worst outcome if you're wrong about being followed by someone, or if you were loud and enforced a boundary?

What Happens If You're Wrong?

Meredith was on a night out with a close friend. It was around Halloween, and they had dressed up as Charlie's Angels. They were walking down a dark street on their way to a party, and Meredith spotted a young guy walking on the other side of the street. Suddenly the guy crossed the street and headed directly towards them. She screamed and grabbed her friend. Surprised by the scream, the stunned guy stopped in his tracks, put up his hands, and replied, "I'm sorry! I'm just trying to cross the street!"

The realization of the misunderstanding had everyone, even the guy, bursting out in laughter. Meredith shared with me that he didn't look scary or suspicious; it was simply dark, he was alone, and they were two girls in pleather pants. An honest misunderstanding with no ill intent on either side quickly becomes apparent. Hopefully, it ends with laughter like Meredith's story. I'm willing to bet that young man NEVER crossed a street towards a group of women again.

If you're worried that enforcing a boundary will offend the other person or that your actions will be called "rude," don't. I'll cover that in the next chapter.

Transition Areas

Transition areas are the space between Point A and Point B. For example, Claudia's transition area was from the bus stop to her apartment. For Ann, it was the mall exit to her car. For Meredith, it was from the car to the party. In these areas, you tend to have the most distractions—you're looking down at your phone to read a text, digging to find your keys in your purse, or talking with someone and not paying attention to your surroundings. They are also the areas in which predators tend to watch for distracted people so they can follow them and wait for the right moment to get what they're after.

During my in-person training sessions, I share a video sent to me by a friend. He made the video while living in a major US city with one of the highest crime rates in the nation.

While walking down a street one rainy night, he noticed a woman walking alone in front of him. As she turned to walk down a narrow passage between two buildings, he noticed the unmistakable white headphone cord going from underneath her hood to the phone in her hand. She was talking to someone. Curious about how long it would take her to realize he was behind her, he started recording video.

The space between the two buildings was just wide enough for one person to walk comfortably. It was a fairly well-lit space with barred windows and an entryway near the end of the building on the left. Across from that entryway and to the right, the passage opened to a large parking area with one light and a few parked cars. When he reached the parking lot and it was obvious she was still not aware of him, he turned off the video and went the opposite direction.

I asked him if he had approached her to let her know he'd been behind her the whole time. He replied, "I didn't because I didn't want to scare her!"

Your sense of hearing is crucial in situational awareness. It works faster than any of your other senses. You can hear in the dark; you can hear around corners and sometimes through walls. You can also hear the footsteps of someone walking behind you. Hearing gets a head start on letting your subconscious know what's in your environment. That's why it's so important not to wear earbuds while walking or running.

However, that doesn't mean you have to stop listening to music or podcasts while outside running or walking. I myself love doing that; it's the precious time in my day I can listen uninterrupted to whatever I want. My solution to keeping my ears open while listening to music is to wear bone-conducting headphones. The sound quality is awesome, yet I can still hear the tags clinking on my dog's collar.

My role isn't to tell you that you can't do something. Instead, I'll help you find ways to do it safely.

While we're under the heading of transition areas, I also need to mention self-defense tools. There are many different options available, but a key point I need you to know is that there is not a single self-defense tool in the world that will protect you when it is at the bottom of your purse, in the center console of your vehicle, or left at your home.

Before leaving your house, getting out of your vehicle, or leaving a building, decide which self-defense tool is best suited for the environment and put it in your hand. If it's Mace® spray, put the spray in your hand. If it's a personal alarm, make sure it's ready to be activated. If it's a tactical flashlight, carry it in the palm of your hand. If it's a firearm or stabbing tool, make sure it's properly stored and easily accessible. If you frequently push strollers or hold little hands while going about your daily routine, make sure you try different tools that fit these situations.

> *There is not a single self-defense tool in the world that will protect you when it is at the bottom of your purse, in the center console of your vehicle, or left at your home.*

Daily Habit: Using Reflective Surfaces

If you think you hear someone following you, a great way to check is by using a reflective surface. Starting tomorrow, look for reflective surfaces in your environment. How many can you spot? Notice what you can see by looking at the reflections in the following:

- Storefronts
- Mirrors
- Sunglasses
- Food cases

- Plexiglass
- Using your phone to fake a selfie
- …what else can you find?

Take a picture of the reflective surface and share it on Instagram with the hashtags #sharpwomen #dailyhabits and make sure to tag @TheDiamondArrowGroup!

I Don't Want to Be Rude!

Say what you feel. It's not being rude, it's called being real.
—Unknown

You know you should be true to yourself, no matter what others think or say. But in real life, it's a challenge a lot of women face. The thought, "I don't want to be rude," often sabotages authentic responses. You can dismantle this thought in two ways.

First, when someone is making you uncomfortable, you have no need to apologize to them—your feeling comes first. Second, being direct is not rude.

Real vs. Rude

- You don't have to apologize to someone who is making you uncomfortable.
- Being direct is not being rude.

The Merriam-Webster Online dictionary defines rude as "being in a rough or unfinished state," "lacking refinement or delicacy," or "marked by or suggestive of lack of training or skill."[10]

Reading that definition makes my face scrunch. It's not a word I would want my behavior associated with! Recognizing the difference between being "direct" and being "rude" will go a long way in sharpening your communication skills.

No Cookies for Sale

Grace and I had met for coffee to discuss business. As we stopped to say our goodbyes outside the main entrance, a guy walked up to us and tried to start a conversation.

"Are you two selling Girl Scout cookies?"

"No," I replied, deadpan, and turned back to our conversation, ignoring him. I could see he was just trying to break the ice, but we were busy talking.

He didn't get the message. "Are you two selling any Girl Scout cookies!?" he asked again.

"No," I repeated

"Geesh, lady, I was just trying to start a conversation."

"Yep." I wasn't going to be drawn in by being forced to apologize, either.

The guy walked away, and Grace and I both laughed.

Listen—I'm not here to judge anyone for their life choices, but it was 9 a.m., and he had a brown-bagged bottle of alcohol in his hand. He had walked up to two women he didn't know and thought it would be okay to interrupt our conversation. Neither of us was obviously selling cookies. And it doesn't matter whether he had ill intent or not; we had no obligation to make conversation with a stranger who was trying to interrupt ours.

---

[10] "Rude," Merriam-Webster Online Dictionary, accessed October 27, 2021, https://www.merriam-webster.com/dictionary/rude.

My responses weren't rude; they were direct.

This correlates with setting and enforcing boundaries, which I will get into in the next chapter. For now, I want you to think about how people use your default of kindness against you.

The 'Startle Factor'

Steve Kardian's book, *The New Superpower for Women: Trust Your Intuition, Predict Dangerous Situations, Defend Yourself from The Unthinkable,* gives another example of a person manipulating kindness against women. Years ago, after several high-profile sexual assaults on college campuses, *Inside Edition* asked him to do a segment, "Are college women too trusting?" It was believed that female college students were not careful enough and put themselves in unsafe situations by letting their guard down too quickly.

In my opinion, another aspect of human behavior that is especially strong in women is the role of caretaker. It's why many experts suggest telling your children that if they are separated from you and need help, they should look for a female, especially one with kids. Women want to help those in need, and predators are happy to use that against us.

An excerpt from Steve's book illustrates this all too well.

> It was September, and the fall term had just begun. Students carrying backpacks were hurrying across the quad to classes or to the library. I had placed myself on the side of one of the large parking lots that dotted campus. Selectively I scanned the women who were walking by. I identified the ones who were unaware of their surroundings, lost in thought, talking on cell phones, or even eating lunch on the go. I looked at posture and stride, getting into the predator mindset. Research shows that in sexual assault cases, looks and outfits are irrelevant. Whether she's tall or short or wearing a miniskirt or sweats, none of that matters. Predators are most often solely interested in a woman who presents as a soft target.
>
> Many people did spot me as out of place and decades too old, even with my quick student disguise of a backpack, baseball hat, and

knee-length shorts. But just as many didn't even bother giving me a second glance. Walking right past me, their gaze lowered, texting or emailing. Or with the ubiquitous buds in their ears-chatting on the phone, listening to music. Or some combination of the above.

Of the women who were distracted and startled when I approached them, I managed to get eight out of eight to let me into their cars by simply saying, "Hey there, could you drop me off at the security gates so I could get some help here?" and motioning in a vague way, as if towards my stalled vehicle.

That was all it took for them to let a stranger into their car.[11]

When I share Steve's story in my training sessions, mothers with teenage daughters about to head off to college visibly shudder. Have you thought about what you would do if a stranger startled you, apologized for startling you, and then asked for your help?

If a stranger surprises or startles you, you will instinctually react with whatever characteristic you most want others to see in you. If you want others to see you as kind, caring, and helpful, that will be your reaction. If you want others to see you as a Sharp Woman and not someone to be messed with, how can you respond with kindness AND boundaries? Another factor in this situation is whether the person is a stranger or someone you know.

If you want others to see you as a Sharp Woman and not someone to be messed with, how can you respond with kindness AND boundaries?

If you've picked up this book in hopes that you can increase your personal safety skills simply by shouting, "No! Get back!" every time someone startles you, I'm about to burst your bubble. Situational awareness is more complex than that. Here are two of my own huge "aha" moments.

---

[11] Steve Kardian, *The New Superpower for Women: Trust Your Intuition, Predict Dangerous Situations, Defend Yourself from the Unthinkable*, (New York: Touchstone, 2017), p. 63-64.

I Am Woman; Hear Me Roar!

I've strived to carry myself as a woman who is not to be messed with. I've been told that I'm intimidating, and people are afraid to say something they think might upset me. My best friend since college still laughs when she tells this story.

We were walking across campus to get to class. A car was slowly approaching us as we stepped off a curb onto a crosswalk. She paused mid-stride, but I kept walking. Realizing the car was stopping to let us cross, she ran to catch up to me.

"Weren't you afraid you were going to get hit by that car?"

My eighteen-year-old-and-indestructible self responded with a shrug. "If they hit me, I'm going to leave a big dent in their car."

In my mind, I was unbreakable. "Don't mess with me" was my default attitude, and it served me well.

Years after that crosswalk experience (and with maturing views of mortality), my default characteristic shifted to wanting to be seen as kind, caring, and helpful. The impact of that shift on my personal safety gave me a wake-up call many years later, as can be seen in the next story.

Maybe I'm Not So Tough After All

Our mail carrier is always friendly when he brings packages to our front door. I work from home, so I'm usually available to accept the delivery. Our Great Dane, Leonidas, acts like he will bust through the door and attack anyone who rings our doorbell. I typically shut him in my office before opening the front door. On a particularly hot summer day, the mail carrier approached our house with a package and two empty water bottles.

As he handed me the package, he asked, "Would you mind filling my water bottles? It's so hot, and the delivery truck doesn't have air-conditioning."

"Of course! I'll get them filled up right away."

I turned around to go back into the house. In the reflection of the hallway mirror, I saw him start following me in.

My first split-second thought was, *What the hell is he doing following me into the house?!?* The next thought quickly followed: *What is the closest thing I could use as a weapon?*

You know what I didn't do? I didn't turn around and tell him to wait outside. I teach situational awareness and boundary enforcement for a living, yet my desire to be kind overruled the priority of my personal safety. I was letting someone I only knew as our mailman enter our house while our 180-pound dog was locked in my office. And I had no self-defense tools on me. Ugh ….

I angled my body so I could keep my eyes on him while filling his water bottles. Our kitchen is a straight, short walk from the front door. When I had filled his water bottles, I made sure he walked ahead of me out the door.

I want to be abundantly clear about our mail carrier: He is a cheerful person who is excellent at his job. Do I think he had any ill intent when he walked into our house? I do not. However, the incident helped me realize a weak point in my personal safety skills. My boundary-enforcement skills were weaker with someone I knew.

What I Would Tell Myself

You and I are human. We will make mistakes. As a coach, I don't believe in berating you or making you feel stupid for making a mistake. I'm here to help you sharpen your skills, not break you. If a client came to me with this story, I would first comment on her good defensive mindset points: tracking his movements in the mirror, looking for potential weapons, staying calm, angling her body to keep an eye on him, and letting him walk out in front of her. Then I would ask why she didn't tell him to stay outside while she filled the water bottles. That would help identify the weak point to prevent it in the future. Yet it's nothing to criticize someone for.

Remember: there is no perfect prescription for safety. If you make a mistake, take note of it, and then get curious about yourself. Why did or didn't you do something? What will you do differently in the future? My role is to act as a guide, not a dictator telling you what you should or shouldn't do. I'm here to help you understand why and then adjust.

Upon reflection, I realized I didn't tell him to stay outside because his entering our house startled me. Instead, I instinctively reacted by being kind and helpful because I knew him and wanted him to see those things in me. I say "knew him" because he wasn't a completely random stranger to me. He had delivered many packages over the years, so my brain put him in the acquaintance category of people in my life. It was an "aha" moment for me. I knew I had zero hesitation enforcing my boundaries with a stranger, but I had a huge glitch in my enforcement if I knew the person. That realization was a lesson I could apply to sharpen my personal safety skills.

Maybe you don't need to worry about a scenario that involves a mail carrier entering your house. Have you ever impatiently waited for an elevator? Have you ever pushed the call button multiple times (because that magically makes them arrive faster, right)? The second the arrow lights up indicating which elevator is arriving, you rush to stand in front of its closed doors.

It's about time! You think. *It's been a long day, and I just want to get to my car, drive home, and put on my comfy clothes.*

When the elevator doors open, a guy standing in the back corner looks you up and down. Your intuition alarm bells go off in your head. Something about this guy gives you the creeps!

In less than a second, your intuition, a natural survival instinct, has sent you a warning message via the shiver that went down your spine.

Something about his presence startled you as the doors opened. Are you going to ignore the signal your intuition is sending because you want to be seen as kind and caring? Or are you going to listen to your natural survival instinct and not enter the elevator? This is heuristics in action. One or more of your senses picked up something that is off with the guy in the elevator. Your subconscious filter looked at that information and decided it was worth passing along to your consciousness via an intuition signal. Your subconscious doesn't have time to tell you exactly what your senses picked up (your eyes seeing him look you up and down, your ears hearing a quiet chuckle, your nose smelling alcohol). It needs you to take action.

That all takes place in the first half-second. The remaining half-second is your brain frantically searching your mental plan "files" for how to react. If you haven't thought about what you would do or say in this elevator scenario before, you will spend more time in an indecisive loop in your brain.

Should I get on the elevator? Should I not get on the elevator? Should I say something about not getting on the elevator? Should I just turn around and not say anything? I don't want to be rude! Ahhh!

The mental back-and-forth ping-pong game is going 100 mph in your head, but you appear frozen in time on the outside. I've heard many instructors say your body can't go where your mind hasn't. That's why going through mental scenario games in your head before you find yourself in a situation is an important part of sharpening your personal safety skills. I'll talk more about building your file cabinet of mental plans in chapter 7.

For now, let's finish talking through this elevator scenario.

So … what would you do?

The key factor in this question is YOU. It doesn't matter what I would do. It doesn't matter what someone else would do. All that matters is deciding what you would do. Because if what I tell you to do is not something that feels natural to you, you won't do it in the moment. Here are some examples of how other women have answered that question during training sessions.

"Is this elevator going up/down? It's not? Oh! Wrong elevator then."

"Oh my gosh! I left the coffee pot on!"

"Oops, I forgot I gave up riding elevators for Lent!"

Then turn and walk away quickly.

The last example is great to use any time of year because it's so random that the guy in the elevator will still be trying to process what you said as the doors close.

Or say nothing at all. Simply turn around and get to safety—making sure he isn't getting off the elevator and following you.

Practice saying it in a doorway of your home. Try out your idea the next time you're about to get on an elevator (even if no one else is in the elevator). Play around with words, your tone of voice, your physical movements. Yes—personal safety is a serious matter, but learning and building your skills can and should involve play. Educators incorporate play when teaching new concepts to students because it makes learning fun, and the lessons stick.

Here's another example that almost all women have experienced at some point—a seemingly kind and generous offer that has strings attached.

Can I Buy You a Drink?

Ann and Bridgette were both newly divorced and had decided to go out for drinks and commiserate about their situations. They went to a local bar and grabbed a table for two. After they had shared some laughter and a few tears over stories of the challenge of being newly single and co-parenting, their drinks were almost empty. A man approached their table, apologized for interrupting, and said he noticed that they seemed to be sharing stories that were deep with emotion. He mentioned that he had experienced hard times too, and he wanted to do something nice to cheer them up. He offered to buy the next round of their drinks. Both friends appreciated his sentiment and accepted. The man walked away from their table and let the bartender know to send over two more drinks. Ann and Bridgette commented that maybe nice guys do exist, and there was hope for them. Kindness offered; kindness accepted. No strings attached.

I'm guessing you know exactly where this is heading.

The no strings attached wasn't actually true. The guy took their acceptance of his drink offer as an invitation for further conversation. When the drinks came, he pulled up a third chair to their table and sat down.

Think back to the story of the man asking my friend and me about selling Girl Scout cookies. This guy interrupted two friends, obviously in a deep conversation, and made a kind gesture of buying their next round of drinks. However, Ann and Bridgette's acceptance did not obligate them to anything. If you've had zero contact (not even eye contact) with a stranger and they offer to buy you a drink, why are they approaching you? This is not a question to ask with a fearful undertone in your head; it's about being curious about his intentions.

You could say, "Well, that's very kind of you. What made you pick us to be the lucky recipients of an all-expense-paid drink?" His response to that question will tell you a lot and help you decide whether or not there is any hidden agenda behind the offer.

Then you can decide if you want to accept the offer. Was your intent for the evening to go out with your friend to enjoy good conversation, or was it to go out and meet new people? That intent should dictate your response. If you've thought about this before leaving your house, it will make handling the situation much easier. A guy interjecting himself into a conversation between two women he doesn't know is crossing a social boundary. It's easily forgiven if the guy has no ill intent and apologizes for any interruption. Be direct; your response can maintain politeness but shouldn't leave room for guessing on his part.

"Sorry to interrupt, but I couldn't help but notice you two might be going through some hard times. I've been there. Can I buy your next round of drinks?"

"That's kind of you. We definitely needed some time to be alone and talk."

"Well, I'll let the bartender know and leave you two alone. I hope things get better."

This is one example of a potential conversation in this situation. It's based on how I would respond and what I would feel comfortable saying. You need to decide what you would do and say in a similar situation.

Being curious and asking questions will help you get to the other person's intent. It's similar to the advice of how to handle a question you don't want to answer.

"Why did you decide to do X?"

"That's an interesting question. Why do you ask?"

Mental Pre-conversation

Have you ever played a conversation over and over in your head before it's even happened? Maybe it's thinking about how you're going to talk to a family member about something you've been wanting to tell them. Maybe it's a work presentation, and you're thinking through all the potential questions people might ask so you can have a good answer prepared.

Mentally practicing conversations to learn the other person's intentions is similar. For instance, if they said this, you would say that—and so on.

Daily Habit: What Would You Say?

Play "What would you say?" in a variety of situations. Make sure to actually say the lines out loud to hear yourself saying them. Work on balancing humor, sarcasm, and tact. It has to be something you would actually say and feels natural to you. Keep it clear and direct. Remember the golden rule: No one likes to be laughed at or talked down to. You don't have to be rude to get your point across.

To get you started, here are some example situations:

- Can I buy you a drink?
- Can I borrow your phone to make a call?
- Would you mind filling my water bottle?
- Do you live around here?
- Do you have kids?
- My hands are too big to put this fuse in. Would you mind helping me with the fuse box in my trunk?

What would be your response in these and other situations?

BONUS QUESTION: Does your response change depending on whether or not you know the person asking you?

Try your lines in real situations! Make sure to share the conversation on Instagram with the hashtags #sharpwomen #dailyhabits and tell us how it went—and don't forget to tag @TheDiamond ArrowGroup!

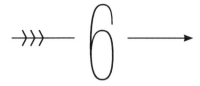

Persistence Is Not
Always a Good Thing

Even to me the issue of "stay small, sweet, quiet, and modest"
sounds like an outdated problem, but the truth is that women still
run into those demands whenever we find and use our voices.

—Brené Brown

Lydia is an intelligent, Sharp Woman who has always had a love for telling stories. Her humor and intellect shine through every word she writes. You can't help but be sucked in, wanting to know what happens next. Many people have told her to write a book, and she smiles and says, "Oh, it will happen!" She has amazing communication skills, so it was beyond comprehension how one man just couldn't seem to understand her "no."

The First Date

Living in a smaller city didn't provide many potential suitor options for Lydia. On first dates, she could figure out pretty quickly whether there would be a second date or not. One man was nice, and they enjoyed a good conversation over dinner, but she didn't feel any chemistry. Lydia made it clear that while she enjoyed talking with him, she wasn't interested in pursuing a relationship beyond a friendship. Somehow her direct honesty didn't compute with the man, and he continued to ask her out on romantic dinner dates. Every time she turned him down and reminded him that she wasn't interested in him that way, she thought he was getting the message. Instead, he started sending flowers to her work. The first bouquet she brushed off as a kind gesture. With his change in tactics, she thought he was finally getting the message.

But the flowers kept arriving at her work. She finally reached the end of her patience and insisted that he stop sending flowers. She then went a step further, telling him his behavior and lack of respect for her boundaries were unacceptable. She did not wish to continue a friendship with him. Lydia had grown more annoyed with every flower delivery.

Persistence Is Stalking

She also grew annoyed by the comments from her co-workers. Most of the women she worked with were married and complained they hadn't been sent flowers from their husbands for years. They were projecting their wants on Lydia, trying to make her feel bad for not wanting to accept what they wished was happening to them. Never mind the fact that the circumstances were completely different. After another unwelcomed bouquet of flowers arrived, one co-worker's comment finally tipped Lydia over the edge.

"He's so sweet! Look at that beautiful arrangement! You should really stop being so rude and give him another chance."

"No—it's not sweet; it's stalking and harassment. I will not be giving him another chance."

I know the saying "persistence is key" is popular in the motivational world. But when the persistence comes from a guy you've told directly and clearly to stop a behavior, it's creepy. It's harassment.

Another perspective shift I love from the book *Gift of Fear* is on the word "charm."

> Charm is another overrated ability. Note that I called it an ability, not an inherent feature of one's personality. Charm is almost always a directed instrument, which, like rapport building, has motive. To charm is to compel, to control by allure or attraction. Think of charm as a verb, not a trait. If you consciously tell yourself, "This person is trying to charm me," as opposed to "This person is charming," you'll be able to see around it. Most often, when you see what's behind charm, it won't be sinister, but other times you'll be glad you looked.[12]

When I read that, it was a palm to the forehead moment. Has another person ever flattered you with compliments, and though you were slightly embarrassed by the praise, you secretly loved the attention?

"Finally! Someone sees and appreciates my efforts!"

As you took a moment to soak in all the warm, fuzzy feelings you were experiencing, the next words out of their mouths involved some sort of sales pitch or ask.

In an instant, the flattery becomes slimy. You feel tricked. You're embarrassed to realize the person's cheesy line pulled you in! You try to hide your humiliation with a few angry words (or maybe just a look that could kill), and you storm away. This type of bait and switch happens to women at an early age experiencing "mean girl" antics. The best friends you made knotted string bracelets for are suddenly making fun of you on the playground. The people involved are different, but the feelings are the same.

---

[12] De Becker, *Gift of Fear*, 57-58.

"How did I fall for it?!?" you ask yourself. "I'm never going to trust when people are complimentary to me again!"

Why Can't You Just Accept a Compliment?

In my opinion, this is where it begins for women not being able to take a compliment at face value. It's easy to be skeptical of praise from friends, family, and even co-workers because you're looking for the ulterior motive behind it. The bait-and-switch game is one that little kids use to get what they want before they realize it's not a healthy way to go about it. They see that when they do or say something nice, they tend to get their way. But that's all the further it goes. They don't have the emotional maturity to understand that **manipulating** kindness to get their way is not okay.

"How do you ask Aunt Lisa for a treat?" their parent prompts.

"Can I please have a treat, Aunt Lisa?" the child responds, and Aunt Lisa gives him a treat.

The inadvertent lesson is that if you use manners and kindness to ask for what you want, the other person is obligated to give it to you.

I'm not saying kids shouldn't learn manners or that you shouldn't reward them for using manners. This is a simple example of how social mores taught at an early age subconsciously impact our whole lives, especially for women. Predators know that. They know they can use charm to manipulate your kindness. You will feel more obligated to fulfill their request because they are asking nicely. Ted Bundy was known for using charm as a tactic to lure his victims. He separately lured two sunbathing women at a public beach to his vehicle by manipulating their kindness and desire to help others in need. He put one arm in a sling and asked them for help getting his sailboat in and out of the water.

Sharpen your curiosity skills. What type of person decides it would be a good idea to go solo-sailing with an injured arm? Why would a grown man ask a woman in a swimsuit for help on a crowded beach with other men around? And let's be real for a moment—when has a man ever thought to himself, "Hmmm, I have something large, heavy, and awkward to move. Let me go ask a woman for help." I'm not saying women aren't capable of lifting large, heavy, awkward items! But thinking about the situation in general, it's not a realistic request.

That's what Gavin de Becker means about taking a moment to look behind the charm. It's pausing to ask yourself, why is this person using charm to get my attention? Most of the time, the person is being complimentary or using manners to make an innocent request. But sometimes, he has ill intent, and you'll be glad you took the time to be curious.

Another time the line between charm and manipulation gets blurry is at the beginning of a new relationship. One person initiates a conversation, using all the charm and wit they can muster to get your attention. They will be on their best behavior and try to say and do all the right things to keep your attention. Many women first encounter this courting in their teenage years.

Ahh, young love. The teenager's hormonal changes bring a rush of the body's natural chemicals—dopamine, oxytocin, and serotonin—at unregulated levels, leading to the emotional rollercoaster so many people experience in their first relationships. This is a broad and deep topic with many different psychological factors, so I'll use a very generic example to stay on point.

The emotional rush of your first love is addicting. You've never felt this way about ANYONE before! You want to spend all your time with them and do everything together! Looking back at this time as adults, we see the fault in that way of thinking. Spending all your time with one person is co-dependency.

I'm guessing you have experienced the emotional rollercoaster in a new relationship at one time in your life. Every little gesture seemed romantic and wonderful, and you felt on top of the world.

But with the highest of highs comes the lowest of lows, and the breakup hits hard. An interesting part of the aftermath of a breakup is the tendency to only think about the good times. The positive feelings during those good times get exaggerated in your memory, and you crave the rush you felt. The craving for affection and attention is so powerful that narcissists and abusers can sense it. At the beginning of Daria's relationship with Mitchell, he sensed her longing for attention after her first husband's affair.

After a romantic relationship ends, you crave those good-feeling chemicals even more. It's why rebound relationships are a thing. After a hard breakup, you may not stop to ask yourself if your new crush is showing love or love-bombing you. *Psychology Today* defines love-bombing as "the practice of overwhelming someone with signs of adoration and attraction."[13]

Love-bombing is a form of manipulation that masquerades as healthy love to control someone's behaviors. I'm not saying you have to be paranoid about all romantic gestures, but pay attention to when and how someone makes them. Does the person have hidden expectations behind the gestures? Thinking back to Lydia's story, the repeated flower deliveries held the underlying expectation that she would eventually give in and agree to go on a date she had already refused.

> *Love-bombing is a form of manipulation that masquerades as healthy love to control someone's behaviors.*

Trying to emotionally manipulate someone under the guise of romantic gestures is creepy. When it happens to you, you can't always articulate why your intuition alarms are going off, especially when people around you only see it from their

---

[13] Suzanne Degges-White, "Love Bombing: A Narcissist's Secret Weapon," *Psychology Today*, April 13, 2018, https://www.psychologytoday.com/us/blog/lifetime-connections/201804/love-bombing-narcissists-secret-weapon.

outside perspective. That's also part of the manipulation—getting the people around you to think they are Mr. Wonderful. I need you to remember that your perspective of the situation is real. Other people who don't understand why you are creeped out by the behaviors are not their target.

Abusers don't start with physical blows. They start with small tests of your boundaries. For example, are you willing to cancel plans with your girlfriends because he wants you to stay home with him? The persuasion comes in the form of childish behaviors: whining, pleading, making you feel guilty for honoring the commitment you made to your friends. If that doesn't work, he may try controlling you in subtle ways to isolate you from friends and family. Again—this happens under the guise of "wanting to take care of you." When you ignore or dismiss subtle love-bombing behaviors, they become controlling tactics that are hard to get away from.

My Story

In high school, I got along with a variety of people and had a co-ed friend group. The core group of people remained the same, and the friendships were tested over the years due to dumb teenage drama, but it was a good crew. There were plenty of times I relied on those friendships to help me work through my teenage angst.

In the spring of my senior year, I broke up with the cliche "high school sweetheart." Afterward, a friend decided to set me up on a blind date with her boyfriend's brother right before graduation.

While there weren't fireworks on that first date, we got along and shared mutual friends. We continued hanging out, whether in a big group or on dates. By the time I left for the Army's basic training a month later, we were calling ourselves boyfriend and girlfriend. We wrote letters every week while I was away. When I returned to attend college in the neighboring state, he would drive the five-hour round trip to pick me up and bring me back home. I didn't have a car, so either he had to make the drive, or I rode with a fellow student who was happy to have someone to split gas money.

I can't honestly say I thought much about leaving campus every weekend. This is an example of how our life experiences as children impact our future perspective. When I was younger, my dad's work had kept him away during the week. When he was home on weekends, our family focused on spending time together. My eighteen-year-old self viewed coming home every weekend as totally normal.

Because I didn't have my own vehicle, it was very convenient for my boyfriend to control where I went and who I hung out with while I was home. Since I was gone the summer after graduation and now attended college in another state, many of my high school friendships grew distant. My friend circle shifted to his friends and their girlfriends. By the end of my freshman year at college, my boyfriend proposed. My naïve eighteen-year-old self, looking through the lens of young love, said yes.

Over that summer, plans for my life changed. I made a tough decision to leave the military. I transferred from the out-of-state college to a two-year school near home that I could afford. I moved into an apartment with friends and then later a trailer home on a dairy farm. I could pay rent by working on the farm, leaving more of my paycheck to pay for school. My routine was work, school, work, and spending time with my fiancé and his friends. At the end of that year, I realized I was way too young to get married. Being around my fiancé more regularly made me realize we had very different visions for our future. I had changed. I had a place to live, a job that helped pay for school and a car, and I was enjoying the new college and the people I was meeting there. I was looking forward to a career and traveling before settling down. My fiancé wanted to start a family and have me be a stay-at-home mom.

I broke up with him and gave the ring back. Over the next few months, I was bombarded with comments from friends and family.

"You two were so good together! He is so stable and responsible; there are not many guys out there like that nowadays! Don't you miss hanging out with all of us?"

The comments were based on other people's perceptions of our relationship. I couldn't articulate the increase of his controlling behaviors as our differences became more apparent.

After the breakup, the ex-fiancé had a habit of showing up uninvited on my doorstep. On one occasion, it was a weekend morning, and a male friend was sleeping on the couch. He had made the smart choice not to drive after a night of partying. The ex stormed up the front steps and began pounding on the front door, demanding to know who was inside. Not interested in a confrontation, my friend slipped out the back door while I opened the front door to confront my ex. I don't recall what my ex said to me, but I remember he was furious and accused me of things that were no longer any of his business.

Other than that one volatile incident, he persistently tried to do and say nice things to get me to take him back. He said he saw the error in his ways and that I could have a career and we would travel before kids. They were all empty promises made to manipulate my emotions to get what he wanted. I've only recently discovered there is a term for this behavior. It's called "future faking."

According to *PsychCentral*, future faking "is when a person lies or promises something about your possible future in order to get what they want in the present."[14]

Guess what? It worked.

---

[14] Darius Cikanavicius, "How Narcissists Use Future Faking to Manipulate You," *PsychCentral*, September 16, 2019, https://psychcentral.com/blog/psychology-self/2019/09/narcissist-future-faking#1.

We got back together and were married the following year. Before walking me down the aisle on my wedding day, my dad jokingly asked if I wanted to skip all of it and go across the street for a soda. I've often wondered if that resulted from his intuition alarm bells going off without knowing how to articulate it to me.

While camping with friends and family a month after our wedding, he and I got into an argument. I don't even remember what we were arguing about. What I do remember is his chilling words.

"I never really loved you; I only married you so you'd never leave me."

I was devastated. I felt trapped. When I had previously broken off the engagement, I faced a lot of negative judgment and abandonment by family and friends. It was an awful time in my life. I didn't want to think about how bad it would be for me if we got divorced.

I demanded couples counseling, but he smugly sat in the sessions and finally admitted he was simply placating my desires until I got pregnant. Then I would be forced to stay home as he wanted. Even the counselor ran out of ways to find a compromise between us. She finally said, "You have to decide whether you're going to work this out or get divorced." He leaned back and crossed his arms.

"I'll never make that decision," he said. "I'll never get divorced."

In a surprisingly controlled rage, I stood up and said, "Well, then I'll make that decision. I want a divorce."

And then I stormed out of her office.

We had only been married five months. The aftermath of my decision to get a divorce felt like a nuclear fallout. Family and friends disowned me. I felt shame and embarrassment. In the Catholic religion I had grown up in, divorce was not accepted.

Over the next two years, I fumbled through my day-to-day routine. I used some unhealthy coping mechanisms such as alcohol and avoidance. A while after the divorce, my new boyfriend, his friends, and I encountered my ex and his friends at a bar. As they spewed their verbal assault at me, I clung to my boyfriend's shirt, begging him and his friends not to get in a fight. We never went back to that bar.

During those two years, I had a job at a great company that saw potential in me. They offered to pay for me to go back to school to get my bachelor's degree. Upper management created opportunities for me to grow and learn within the company. Everyone else thought it was the perfect place for me to grow in my career. But it didn't excite me. After going through a nasty divorce and losing so much because I didn't listen to my intuition, I wasn't going to ignore my inner voice again. That's when I pitched the idea of leaving everything behind and moving to California with my best friend from college.

She was all in. We packed only what could fit in our cars. I had $500 in my savings account and no job lined up. We had a place to stay until we got settled. It was one of the best things I ever did for myself. Moving so far from home allowed me to figure out who I was and what was important to me.

'It Won't Happen to Me'

Bright, intelligent, confident women find themselves in horrible relationships all the time because it doesn't start out horrible. If taken at face value, behaviors like persistence and charm aren't considered red flags of a controlling and potentially abusive relationship. No one is perfect, and everyone makes mistakes. Forgiveness and grace are cornerstones of being a good person, especially at the beginning of relationships. You are just getting to know the person. It's easy to see behaviors in a positive light, giving them the benefit of the doubt that they had the best intentions. When Mitchell insisted on handling all the wedding details, he did it under the guise of wanting to take all the stress off Daria so she could enjoy the wedding day.

Have you ever wished for someone else to handle all the party planning details so that all you had to do was relax and enjoy it? Of course! We all want someone to step up and do things to make our lives easier. But if you're getting an intuition signal that something is off about a person's persistence, take a moment to ask yourself the following:

- ♦ What does the other person get out of me giving in to their persistent requests?
- ♦ What do I want in this situation?
- ♦ What is the reaction of the person when I don't go along with their request?

I'm guessing you can look back and see situations where someone was very persistent with you. As you think about those situations, ask yourself whether any people made your intuition alarm bells go off. Did any of them give you a creepy feeling?

Being kind means forgiving honest mistakes. It means you look for the best in people. It does not mean you become a doormat and let them walk all over you. That's why knowing your mental and physical boundaries are so important.

At the end of the day, you are responsible for yourself: your happiness, your dreams, your mistakes, your hardships. Don't let someone who doesn't have to deal with the consequences of your decisions make you feel like you have to do things their way.

Daily Habit: What and Where Are Your Boundaries?

You need to know your boundaries **before** you are in a situation where you need to enforce them. It's much easier to spot a boundary crosser immediately and stop their behavior if you are prepared.

- Do you have a limit on how many nights a week you're willing to allow outside commitments?
- How closely are you comfortable letting people stand next to you?
- Are you okay with receiving hugs?
- What do you need to recharge your batteries? How often do you need that?
- What are your boundaries of doing work outside your typical work hours?
- Who are the people you would answer a middle-of-the-night phone call from?
- Do your boundaries change depending on who the person is?

Make sure to share on Instagram any new boundaries you've established with the hashtags #sharpwomen #dailyhabits—and remember to tag @TheDiamondArrowGroup!

Is That Your Final Answer?

You can be a good person with a kind heart and still say no.
—Lori Deschene

From two-year-olds to bosses, or romantic partners and pushy friends to strangers, you've dealt with people who won't take no for an answer. Being firm when saying no takes practice. The following are important:

- ◆ Say it loudly enough so the other person clearly hears you.
- ◆ Stop yourself from overexplaining why you are saying no.
- ◆ Don't back down from enforcing your boundary.

Many factors play into how you handle a situation with a person who wants to push past "no." For instance, the situation determines options. In the examples from the previous paragraph, you don't have an option to go to HR for your two-year-old. (Although, how nice would it be to file a complaint about insubordination and let someone else deal with your mini-me?)

Kindness Does Not Equal Good Intentions

Chrissy and I were in Australia representing a charity at a fund-raising event. On an open night, we went out to have dinner and check out a local festival. To get back to our hotel afterward, we booked a rideshare. We made small talk with our driver. He correctly guessed we were tourists due to our lack of Australian accents and our questions about the culture. When we reached our hotel, the driver handed back his business card. He said we could call him directly when we needed a ride to the airport. I accepted his card and thanked him. He then asked for our numbers so he would know it was us calling. I declined and said we had his card to contact him.

As Chrissy and I got out of the car, he asked for our numbers again. I firmly stated that we had his card and would call if we needed a ride. When the driver pulled away from the curb, I promptly threw his card in the trash can outside the hotel. In those circumstances, and with our desire to prioritize our safety in a foreign country, we would not be calling him for a ride.

When someone doesn't accept the first no, consider the situation and ask yourself why they are pushing your boundaries. You don't have to spend a lot of time thinking about it. This is a way to sharpen your assessment skills and clarify what you need to do next.

In the case of the Australian rideshare driver, here's how I thought it through:

- There was no reason for him to have our contact information. I had his information in the app, and he had given me his business card.
- He was well aware that we were tourists, and a ride to the airport meant we would be checked out of our hotel.
- Other than the airline ticketing agents, no one would be waiting for us to arrive at the airport.

♦   The preceding factors are important because after checking out, there is a space of time where no one would notice we were missing. In missing-person cases, the longer it takes for someone to notify authorities, the lower the odds of finding the person(s) alive.

If I shared this story outside the context of this book, you might have viewed his persistence through the rose-colored lenses of kindness. It wouldn't make your viewpoint wrong. However, there is no way to know his true intentions. Regardless of whether his intention was kindly or not, you are not obligated to assume kindliness and take the chance of finding out they were not. You also don't need to apologize for prioritizing your own safety over being reciprocally kind and potentially compromising yourself.

I Need Back Up!

The moment your instincts tell you something is off with another person's behavior, wouldn't it be great to have someone else to validate your concerns? You want that confident other voice telling you you're not the only one who's getting a weird vibe.

But others can be wrong or have different boundaries. So ignoring your intuition because someone else seems okay with the circumstances is not a good strategy. Instead, you need to determine your own mental, emotional, and physical boundary lines. Once you clarify those, the next question becomes, how will you enforce them?

The individuals that don't respect your boundaries are not going to quit pushing after the first no. In fact, now that they know where your line is, they may view it as a challenge. It becomes a game to them. If they can get you to change your mind after you've repeatedly said no, it feels like a victory. The next question in their mind becomes, what other boundaries can I break? It's the cliché: if you give a mouse a cookie, it'll want a glass of milk.

In some situations, simply walking away from the boundary pusher is your best option. For instance, is the mall kiosk employee trying to get you to check out their skin-care product? If you keep walking, they will move on to the next shopper.

In other situations, the boundary pusher may be in the same space and can follow you as you walk away. This could be at home, at work, or in a social setting. A small child having a tantrum can simply follow you into the next room and continue pleading. A co-worker begging for your help with a procrastinated project can follow you to your workspace. A stranger trying to engage you in a conversation you don't want could pull up a chair and join you at your table.

You've clearly said no, and you've tried to walk away from the situation. When those don't work, what would you feel comfortable doing next? Depending on the circumstances, you could enlist the help of others to distract the boundary pusher. I've heard stories of women acting like they recognize another woman as an old friend.

"OMG, is that you, Susie? It's so good to see you! How have you been? What's new with you?"

In a social setting, perhaps you can get a manager's or employee's attention and let them know you've asked this person politely to leave you alone. You even tried walking away, but it hasn't worked. If it's another patron of the establishment, the manager can ask them to leave. The boundary pusher may be someone they know well and have had issues with in the past. Making management aware that they are causing issues again gives them a reason to take things to the next level. They could trespass them from the establishment, for example. You have options, and knowing them ahead of time will give you the self-confidence to enforce your boundaries.

So, What Are Your Boundaries?

Hearing someone say, "You need to set boundaries," may sound a lot like, "Fold in the cheese!" You know having boundaries to protect you are important, but what do I mean by boundaries?

Merriam-Webster's Online Dictionary defines boundaries as "something that indicates or fixes a limit or extent."[15]

You may be thinking to yourself, yes—I know what boundaries are, but what type of boundaries are you talking about regarding my personal safety?

An online search for the different kinds of boundaries brings up an overwhelming variety of nuances. Therefore, to summarize these: Boundaries establish who you are and promote a healthy environment for interacting with others. You cannot have a rich and enjoyable life without setting boundaries that protect your physical and mental well-being.

According to Mindbodygreen:

> Healthy boundaries are the ultimate guide to successful relationships. Without healthy boundaries, relationships do not thrive—they result in feelings of resentment, disappointment, or violation. These feelings, unchecked, can lead to being cut off from others or enmeshment, where there's no clear division between you and others' needs and feelings. Neither of these situations is ideal.[16]

Let's understand the different types of boundaries. Here is interesting information I found on the iNLP Center's website:

> Weak emotional boundaries are amongst the most confusing of psychological issues because it is very difficult to self-diagnose weak boundaries.

---

[15] "Boundary," Merriam-Webster Online Dictionary, accessed October 27, 2021, https://www.merriam-webster.com/dictionary/boundary.

[16] Elizabeth Earnshaw, "6 Types of Boundaries You Deserve to Have (and How to Maintain Them)," mindbodygreen, July 20, 2019, https://www.mindbodygreen.com/articles/six-types-of-boundaries-and-what-healthy-boundaries-look-like-for-each.

Because the emotional boundaries (rules, expectations, protocol) that set the stage for our relationships are initially formed when we are very young children, typically between the ages of three to four, whichever boundaries are naturally formed become the reality within which we operate, at least until we mature enough to question it. This usually doesn't happen until our late twenties or early thirties, if it happens at all.

What are emotional boundaries?

Like physical boundaries, emotional boundaries define separateness. Your emotional boundaries are the property lines that separate your thoughts and feelings from those of other people. If you are confused as to where to draw the line, you cannot avoid emotional and relational troubles. It is like living in a crowded neighborhood with a lot of communal property and some private property, with residents having no idea how to distinguish one type of property from the other. Chaos ensues that has no end until the right lines are drawn, rules set, and order established.[17]

Understanding your emotional boundaries and establishing where to set them can be overwhelming, especially if you weren't raised with healthy boundaries in the first place. The rules and expectations around boundaries are introduced when you are too young to understand or question whether they are healthy. This is why patterns of abuse repeat themselves from generation to generation. If you didn't see healthy boundaries growing up, you don't have a model to use in your current life.

Think back again to the definitions of rude from chapter 5. They are negative and not something you want to be associated with your behaviors. If someone says you're being rude, you feel the need to apologize and change your behavior. Even if the person saying it is a complete stranger, your initial reaction is typically embarrassment and shame.

---

[17] Mike Bundrant, "How to Know if You Have Weak Emotional Boundaries," iNLP Center, accessed October 27, 2021, https://inlpcenter.org/weak-emotional-boundaries.

Boundaries in Your Friend Circle

The people in your friend circle should want to help you live a happy, safe, and wonderful life. If they don't, they shouldn't be in your friend circle. No one should get a free pass to abuse your boundaries over and over again under the guise of being a friend.

This emotional response is ingrained in youth from the start—people tell you to use your manners, be polite, be kind, don't make others feel bad. While I'm not saying you shouldn't teach those respectful guidelines to kids, I'm saying you need to be aware that you're not sending the full message. As an adult, you know what you mean, and you assume your kids will understand how to apply respectful boundaries in the right situations. What society fails to explain to parents is that having respectful boundaries for kids is even more important.

Enforcing your boundaries with someone you know can change things exponentially. It's not a stranger calling you "rude" and never seeing you again. With someone you know, you have to deal with the repercussions the next time you see them.

I Thought You Were My Friend

The life expectancy for men is shorter than it is for women. When I look around at most of my closest girlfriends, they are typically a decade younger than their husbands, just like the age gap between my husband and me. My husband likes to joke that we intentionally selected older partners because we all want to live like the friends in *The Golden Girls* after our husbands kick the bucket.

He's not completely wrong. *The Golden Girls* women had a great friendship.

There is no other relationship like the one between you and your best friends. A best friend is someone who will pick up the phone in the middle of the night if it's you calling. She doesn't care how messy your house is when she stops by for chips and hummus. A best friend knows when to sit with you in sadness and celebrate your triumphs.

When a best friend crosses a boundary, you will give her much more grace and forgiveness. She's human, and everyone makes mistakes!

However, that doesn't mean you should just allow it. You still need to answer the question of where your boundaries are in that relationship and how you will enforce them.

Sam and Denise had been friends since high school. Even though they went to different colleges, they had kept in touch over the years. They were in each other's weddings and even threw each other's baby showers. As they got older, it was not unusual for their phone conversations to last hours when they finally had a chance to catch up. Marriage, kids, careers, and living a few hours apart created a natural distance in their friendship. Still, they seemed to be able to pick up where they left off every time they spoke.

Denise wasn't sure of the exact moment when things changed between her and Sam. From her perspective, it happened overnight. Sam was getting a divorce, and figuring out how to divide a household and time with the kids was not going well with her soon-to-be ex-husband. Denise did everything she could to be there for her friend. Unfortunately, having never experienced divorce herself, she didn't always know what to say. It seemed the more Denise and Sam spoke over the phone, the angrier Sam would become. Denise sensed that Sam was grieving the loss of her marriage and projecting her anger onto Denise's marriage instead of processing her emotions healthily. It felt like Sam was trying to find flaws in Denise's husband and bring them up so Denise would start a fight with him.

At first, Denise did have more fights with her husband after having conversations with Sam. It wasn't until her husband pointed out the correlation that she started to realize the friendship's negative impact on her emotional boundaries. When she brought it up to Sam, all she got back was defensiveness and gaslighting. Denise had never considered the possibility that negative behaviors that impacted her boundaries would come from her best friend. It took her a long time and many difficult conversations with Sam before she finally decided the close friendship was over. She would always cherish the good memories, but it was not healthy for her or her marriage to keep close ties.

You have people in your life now that may not be as close to you in the future. A few of those friendships will end up distancing naturally in the changing seasons of life. Some of the friendships will come to an abrupt end because you realize they are draining you. Your mental health is an important part of situational awareness. Abusive behaviors can come from anyone. Focus on the red-flag behaviors that cross your boundaries, not who is delivering them.

Boundaries in Your Work Circle

Think about the males in your work circle for a moment. Whether the circumstance involves asking for help on a project or asking you out on a date, boundaries at work are now more important than ever. Without clear boundaries and a plan to enforce them, you'll have limited options for dealing with difficult situations.

For example, the co-worker who always seems to seek you out for help because they didn't get their work done on time may turn on the charm. Think of charm as a verb and ask yourself, "What's the benefit to them if I back down on enforcing my boundary and agree to help out?" You stayed late to get caught up on your own work while they got to leave early. I'm not saying you should never help a co-worker, male or female, who asks for your assistance once in a while. I'm referring to the repeat offenders who take advantage of your willingness to help them because you don't want to seem rude.

Here's another work situation that men with good intentions often ask me about. They want to know how to be part of the solution and create a safe working environment for their female colleagues.

Bill likes to make sure female colleagues get back to their hotel room safely during work trips. He doesn't want to come off as creepy, so he asked me how to express his genuine concern. My advice to him? Ask the women if they want his help.

You know when a trusted male co-worker is genuinely concerned for your safety. It comes from your intuition and past interactions with him. Bill didn't lack confidence in his co-workers' ability to get back to their hotel rooms safely. He was merely concerned that they might not feel 100 percent safe, and he wanted to help.

You can be a sharp and independent woman with great personal safety skills and still appreciate a sincere concern for your safety. It's not a weakness to accept help.

Boundaries in Your Family Circle

Based on statistics on violence against women, you can predict that a large percentage of the time, you will likely know your attacker. The older you get, the more your time is spent with family. It can be a challenge to enforce boundaries with people you see at every holiday gathering. It becomes even more difficult when they disregard your boundaries. I could tell you to remove them from your life, but that is much easier said than done because they are family. Take Eleanor's story, for example.

Eleanor got weird vibes every time she was around her brother-in-law while spending time with her extended family. He seemed to pay extra attention to her two young boys, always engaging in conversation with them. At first glance, it was easy to shrug off the intuition alarm bells sounding in her head about his behaviors. He was an uncle interacting with his nephews. Wasn't that what uncles were supposed to do? Still, something about the way he interacted with them gave her a weird vibe.

When Eleanor gave birth to a baby girl, the behaviors of the uncle became something more. He seemed to focus a lot of his attention on the new baby. He would offer to help with her a little too much. With Grandma and the other Aunts around, there was no shortage of family members to help if she needed it.

During one family get-together, Eleanor woke up before her baby daughter and decided to take a quick shower. Grandma was downstairs making coffee, and her husband was still asleep. After showering and getting dressed uninterrupted by a hungry baby, she went to the portable crib to check on her. But the crib was empty. Her husband was still asleep in bed. Eleanor assumed the baby must have started fussing while she was in the shower, so Grandma probably scooped her up for snuggles.

On her way to the kitchen, she discovered the uncle was with the baby and not Grandma. The realization gave her a sick feeling in her stomach that she couldn't shake. The uncle awkwardly handed the baby to her and explained he had heard her crying and went in to check on her. He had changed the baby's diaper and was simply waiting for Eleanor to get out of the shower to feed her.

Were his behaviors those of a well-meaning family member just trying to help with a newborn? Or were they crossing a line into inappropriate behavior? There is no perfect answer. You know the history and patterns of behavior of the people around you, but you don't know the same things about other people's families.

This is another reason why trusting your gut when you get a weird feeling about a situation is so important. If you seek validation of your intuition signal from someone else who discounts it, that doesn't mean your intuition was wrong. The other person wasn't there, and they are operating with a different subconscious filter. Your senses picked up signals that your subconscious filter decided needed your attention.

Family members or not, your boundaries are important and should be respected.

Boundaries with Strangers

When working on my personal safety skills, I've found that enforcing my boundaries with strangers is much easier. I don't care what a stranger thinks of me; I'm never going to see them again. Did I offend them because I'm making my safety a priority? I don't care.

I'm not saying all strange men are the problem. In fact, I've found that most men want to help women be safe. It's part of their protective nature. And, if we're going to have real discussions about violence against women, Margaret Atwood's quote needs to preface the conversation.

> *"Men are afraid that women will laugh at them.*
> *Women are afraid that men will kill them."*
> —Margaret Atwood

At a training I was conducting for a small business, the employees were mostly female, with one male named Steve. After the training session, Steve shared a story about a "stubborn woman" who he tried to help. I would describe Steve as a man in his late twenties with a quiet demeanor and a preference for intellectual conversation over wild nights at the bar.

Steve's Perspective

Steve was driving to a customer's location and noticed a car on the side of the road with its hazard lights flashing. It was a two-lane highway without a lot of traffic, and this particular area was more rural. There were not many homes nearby. A woman was trying to break loose the lug nuts, and a spare tire was next to her. He didn't want her stranded and alone without help. He pulled over in front of her vehicle, got out of his car, and started walking towards her. While still a good distance from her, he asked if she needed help.

She stood up and waved him off, saying she didn't need any help. She had called someone, and they were on their way. Steve told me he hadn't believed her and thought she was simply trying to get him to leave. He was slightly offended that she had dismissed him, but he drove off anyway.

While driving back along the same route a little while later, he noticed the car and woman were still in the same spot. He pulled over again. This time, when she said she didn't need any help, he bluntly told her she did and proceeded to finish changing her tire.

In an exasperated tone, he said: "If she had just let me help the first time, she could have been well on her way!"

I told him that if I had been that woman, he might have ended up in the hospital.

Do not misunderstand my reply to Steve. I want to believe chivalry is not dead! A kind man wanting to help a woman stranded on the side of the road is commendable. But his behaviors would be red flags from the perspective of making my safety a priority. Let me retell the story from your perspective as the woman.

You are driving down the road when suddenly, you hear a loud sound, and your steering wheel starts vibrating. You pull over onto the shoulder and turn your hazard lights on. Checking to make sure no cars are coming down the traffic lane, you get out of your car to check out the situation. You're pretty sure you have a flat tire by the sound you heard; now, you just need to figure out which one it is. You start grumbling under your breath because, OF COURSE, this would happen when you had a day full of errands to run.

Ah-ha, the rear passenger tire is flat. You think to yourself, *At least it's on the ditch side; I'm pretty sure I can change this myself.* Even though you're frustrated and not wearing clothes conducive to changing a tire, you're grateful you know how to do it. You get the spare and tire iron out of your trunk and get to work.

While you're cussing about the difficulty of breaking the lug nuts loose, a man suddenly calls out, asking if you need help. You were so focused on the lug nuts that you didn't notice him pull over in front of your car. He looks friendly enough, but it's a road without much traffic, and there aren't many houses around. You've been listening to true crime podcasts and think, *This is how serial killers get their victims! Gah!*

You tell him you're fine and that help is on the way (you want him to think another person will be arriving soon). You notice his slight eye roll as he turns to walk away. It's not that you wanted to come off as rude, but you also don't want to find out if he is a serial killer.

You go back to cussing at the lug nuts.

About twenty minutes later, you've been able to get the spare tire in place, and now you're struggling to get the lug nuts back on. Suddenly, the same man you shooed away is back! You think, *He's definitely a serial killer, and now he's here to kidnap me! Why didn't I call someone to come help me with this stupid tire!* You start to tell him your help was delayed but is just a minute away, but he doesn't stop walking towards you and instead says that he is going to help you right now. You think, *This is how it ends for me!*

He takes the tire iron from your hand, and suddenly you realize you have nothing to defend yourself from getting hit over the head with it. You stand back, but you don't want to take your eyes off of him until you can figure out your next move. Should you start running through the field to get away? You're not wearing the right shoes! Maybe you could get far enough down the road and flag down another passing car. But what if you don't see another vehicle in time?

You are still standing there, frozen, while your mind runs through all these different scenarios. The man stands up, puts the tire iron and flat tire in your trunk, and closes the lid. He wipes his hands on his pants and, with a smirk, tells you to have a good day. He turns to walk back to his car and drives away. You're still standing in the same spot, but now you feel like an awful person for thinking he was a potential serial killer instead of a good Samaritan. You didn't even get to thank him! You smack your forehead with the palm of your hand and chide yourself for letting your mind go crazy with worst-case scenarios. You decide it's time to stop listening to true crime podcasts.

The reality is, it doesn't matter if a guy acts with good intentions. Your perspective of the situation and what it means to your personal safety is what counts. It's a lot like handling a gun. You might know you've unloaded it. You might believe it's empty. But you can never assume it's not loaded. So, for safety reasons, every time you handle it, you treat it as if it's loaded. Incorrectly assuming otherwise *even once* can lead to deadly consequences.

I often hear that men feel bad that the world is the way it is and that women are scared simply by their presence. They know they have good intentions and want to be seen as a good guy. I understand their point. However, insisting that you need their help because they have good intentions doesn't mean squat if they disregard your boundaries. Insisting you are helpless and need them to fix things is condescending. It's like telling a child they can't do something without letting them try first. You learn by the struggle of trying new things.

I'm not saying you have to go through a blowout to learn how to change a tire. That is the same as saying you have to go through being attacked to learn situational awareness skills. When you want to learn a new skill, you need to practice doing it. (You're reading this book, so that's a step in the right direction. Yay!)

As I mentioned before, I want to believe chivalry is not dead. I want men to offer assistance to you if they see you struggling with something. Men also need to believe you when you say you don't want their help. That is respecting your boundaries. By forcing their assistance, they convey that they think you're either too incompetent to do it or too dumb to realize you need help. Again—red-flag behaviors of trampling your boundaries. If you turn them down, I want them to show respect for your wishes. So what if it takes you longer to change a flat tire than it would take them? I want to celebrate with you as you triumph over your struggles and gain a new skill!

It's not about them; it's about you building your self-confidence in your own abilities to be a Sharp Woman.

> *"When you strengthen one area of your life,*
> *it will spill over into strengthening others as well."*
> —Evy Poumpouras

Daily Habit: Your Mental Strategy File Cabinet

At the end of the last chapter, you took the time to figure out your mental and physical boundaries. Now you need to decide how you would enforce them.

- What would you say to a person standing too close to you in a public space?
- How would you respond to a question you didn't want to answer?
- If the person testing your boundaries continues to persist, what would you say next?

- Would your responses change depending on your relationship with the person testing your boundaries? For instance, compare being at work, at home, with friends, or in public with a complete stranger.
- If the boundary pusher is not listening to your words, what is your next move?
- Who would you feel comfortable enlisting help from to get away from a boundary pusher?

Use Instagram to share any witty comebacks you come up with—use the hashtags #sharpwomen #dailyhabits, and make sure to tag @TheDiamondArrowGroup!

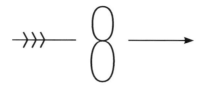

What's My Obligation?

*We cannot change what we are not aware of, and once
we are aware, we cannot help but change.*

—Sheryl Sandberg

n all of my emergency preparedness training, I've heard the same
rule of thumb repeated over and over again: "Take care of yourself
first before assisting others."

You can probably think of many cliché sayings as examples of this.

"You can't pour from an empty cup."

"Put on your own air mask before assisting others."

"You can't give love to others if you don't love yourself first."

Putting yourself and your personal safety needs first may be
one of the hardest things you have to learn along your situational
awareness journey. It's not about being selfish; it's about recognizing you matter. Your safety matters. You can define personal space
and decide what behaviors are acceptable to you. It's speaking up
and using your voice to enforce boundaries. It's realizing you are
responsible for putting your safety first.

Social Media

This topic is like Pandora's box. I hesitate even to lift the lid to start the discussion, but NOT including some basic guiding principles to protect your personal safety would be a disservice to you.

First, remember that you are under no obligation to post personal photos, share your opinions, or talk about intimate details of your life online.

You can decide to share any of the things I just mentioned. I'm not saying you can't. However, I'm asking you to prioritize your personal safety when doing so. Remember: this is a public platform that will live on in cyberspace for an undetermined amount of time. Just as people don't wake up in the morning expecting to be victims of violent crimes, they also don't anticipate how publicly sharing private information could come back to haunt them. Unfortunately, when you're living life, sharing your mistakes, and being authentic, the public forum can be unforgiving. We've seen it over and over again. Posts shared years or even decades ago can impact your current professional and personal life.

Should I Connect with Them?

Depending on the platform, there are many ways to connect with strangers on social media. Do some detective work before you accept or ask to connect with them. Do you have mutual friends? If so, why haven't you met them in person before? If the person is in your career field, ask one of those mutual friends about them. If you have zero mutual connections, ask yourself why they want to connect with you. (This is similar to the thought process for questioning why a person would be trying to charm you.)

A basic rule to start with is, "No eyeballs, no friendship." Meaning, if you haven't ever met them in person, don't connect with them on your personal social media accounts. I've heard too many catfishing stories to trust random connection requests.

Merriam-Webster defines the verb "catfish" as "to deceive (someone) by creating a false personal profile online."[18]

It's effortless for a person with ill intentions to create a fake profile to connect with you for a variety of motives, from relatively innocent to downright nefarious. All they need to do is create an email and set up a profile. People can create any type of persona, even pretending to be members of the opposite sex to try and get you to let your guard down. One trick I use when researching profiles is to check when the profile was created. Has it been around for years, or was it created recently? Along with the profile creation date, you should consider several other factors before accepting a connection request from a person you don't know.

For instance—is this a business or personal connection? I sometimes accept connection requests from strangers on my business-focused social platforms because I'm building my network to reach more of my target market. However, my personal platforms are different, and I'm much more selective of who I connect with and what I post there.

Send Me a Picture!

The addition of cameras on cell phones is both a blessing and a curse—especially when those cell phones are connected to the internet. You can share photos with family and friends easily and quickly. You no longer have to wait until the roll of film is full, take it to a store to get it developed, and drive back to pick it up. You can snap a selfie with the gorgeous sunset in the background and send it all around the world in seconds. Your friends can ask for pictures of your completed home remodel project to see how it turned out. If you're trying to figure out what to wear to an event,

---

[18] "Catfish," *Merriam-Webster Online*, accessed October 29, 2021, https://www.merriam-webster.com/dictionary/catfish.

it's easy to ask your friend for their top pick of your outfit choices by sending photos. It's become normal to take pictures of anything and everything in your everyday life. When it comes to your personal safety, it's important to know your boundaries on what images you share. Here's a great example of odd behaviors around social platforms and photo requests.

Roxy was in her senior year of high school. She used one main social platform to share funny moments and stay connected with friends. On a different platform, a boy she didn't know in person had connected with her through her friends. When he also requested to connect with her on the platform she used more often, she accepted.

She thought the boy may have a crush on her because he always responded to her public posts with likes and hearts and complimented the new outfits she showed off to the friend group. Nothing about these typical teen crush behaviors sounded any alarms in her head—until he started asking for pictures of her.

On the main social forum where she connected with friends, she took photos and videos within the platform and sent them directly. It wasn't typical to take photos from a camera roll and share them. Any time she took a picture, she shared it immediately through the social platform. When the boy asked to see a picture of her wearing the new outfit she had told the friend group about, something seemed off about the request. She brushed it off by telling him she still had to take the tags off of it. When the boy started asking for other photos of her, complimenting her looks, she decided to turn the tables to test his intentions. Roxy asked him to send a photo of himself to her.

When he refused by saying, "You don't want to see a picture of me; I'm ugly," her intuition alarm bells went off. She went back to his profile and realized most of the photos he shared were of other things. None featured himself.

Could he truly have had low self-esteem about his looks? Maybe. The important thing to stress in this situation is she has no obligation to send him photos of herself directly. She shared pictures with the whole friend group when she wanted to, without any obligation to send him individual photos. Did Roxy have a responsibility to help the boy feel better about himself by trying to build his self-esteem? Absolutely not. Yes, I believe the world needs kind people, but never let anyone guilt you by using kindness as a manipulation technique.

This is such a key thing: Anytime anyone asks you for something that makes you uncomfortable, ask yourself, *What's my obligation?*

In reality, the only obligation you have regarding personal safety is making it your priority. The other person's response to the enforcement of boundaries that make your safety a priority says more about them than it does you.

> *Anytime anyone asks you for something that makes you uncomfortable, ask yourself,* What's my obligation?

Arguing You out of 'No'

Do you like being told no? As a Sharp Woman, you probably didn't get where you are by waiting for permission to go after what you want. There are so many motivational quotes on not taking no for an answer or breaking through any limitations placed on you. Women get these messages over and over again in their careers. Is it any wonder applying the messaging gets messy when it comes to enforcing boundaries?

Hollywood glamorizes the persistence and determination of Romeo pursuing Juliet. The other ladies of the court swoon and wish they had a persistent Romeo chasing them. **sigh**

I'm not against romantic gestures, don't get me wrong! However, I believe society's conversation around these gestures needs to include obligation. Thinking back to Lydia's story in chapter 6, her co-workers thought the continued flower deliveries to her work were a romantic gesture. They tried to convince her to change her mind about accepting a second date from the man, even though she had told them she didn't want to. Just because someone does something society views as romantic, you are under no commitment to do anything on your part. Being gracious and thanking someone for an act of kindness is one thing. Feeling obligated to a guy who has repeatedly ignored your boundaries while trying to wear you down using tactics labeled "romantic" by social mores is another.

A gift given with pure intentions of thoughtfulness should not include strings of obligation. If there are strings attached, it's not an altruistic gift.

When Ann and Bridgette accepted the drink from the seemingly nice gentlemen in chapter 5, they had no obligation to let him join them at their table. The "let me buy you a drink" pick-up line is widely used on the dating scene because it works. It's a great way to start a conversation between two single people mutually looking to connect with another person. There is no obligation; it's a shared goal of starting a conversation with someone you're interested in. What happens when only one person is interested in the conversation?

Have you ever been pressured to have a conversation with someone you weren't interested in talking to? Did they offer to do something nice for you, like buy your drink? Or maybe you were in line at the coffee shop, and they insisted on paying for your order. You didn't want to feel obligated to have a conversation with them, so you politely turned them down with a simple, "no thanks."

But the persistent person wasn't going to take no for an answer! Instead, maybe they called you uptight. They may have even tried to make you feel guilty.

"Oh, you're one of those high-maintenance women who need to be wined and dined before you'll talk to someone."

In these types of scenarios, I use my sarcasm and humor to agree with them, leaving them nothing to work with. There's a fine line between using sarcasm to offend someone and using it to make them laugh. Remember that Margret Atwood quote? Men are afraid women will laugh at them. The goal is not to poke the bear and escalate the situation; it's to say something that distracts and ends the conversation so you can walk away.

"You are so uptight; it's just a drink!"

"Exactly! I keep my core engaged so I can walk around more easily."

You've started to work on thinking of one-liner responses from the Daily Habit exercise in chapter 5. Now, use that same skill to think of responses for these scenarios. To make these answers really successful, ensure they don't correlate to their back-handed compliment. Being uptight has nothing to do with engaging your core muscles in that situation, but while his brain tries to process your response because he wasn't expecting it, you'll be five steps away. This is a way to handle the situation, whether the person trying to guilt you is a man or a woman. Work on coming up with some verbal curveballs to throw at anyone who's trying to guilt you into changing your mind.

Now, what should you do if someone gets angry with you for turning them down?

First of all, if any guy ever gets angry because you've said no to him, that's a very, very, very HUGE red flag. You have zero obligations to anyone who makes you feel uncomfortable by their behaviors.

Second, remember that their response to your boundary enforcement says everything about them and nothing about you.

Third, stay calm.

If they respond with anger because you don't want to accept their offer, you don't

If any guy ever gets angry because you've said no to him, that's a very, very, very HUGE red flag.

need to feel obligated to change your mind to get them to calm down. Instead, keep yourself calm. Depending on the situation, repeat that you don't want another drink, or you don't want them to pay for your order. If their anger continues to escalate, consider asking the server or barista to get a manager. (If they've been paying attention, you may not even need to ask; the manager may already be on the way.) A great program called the SAFE Bar Network partners with bars and other alcohol-serving venues to teach all staff how to work together in bystander intervention.

Unless a circumstance causes you to feel you must leave the establishment, stay put. The last thing you want is an angry person following you out to a parking lot where you will be alone with them or where their friends are waiting.

You Don't Have to Be Florence Nightingale

It is wonderful to have a kind, generous, caring heart with a willingness to help other people. The world would be a better place if society focused on making those characteristics a sign of success. As a Sharp Woman, you have those characteristics and use them to take care of people you love. The last thing I want this book to do is make you feel like you have to stop doing that to stay safe.

What I want you to do instead is build a habit of asking yourself, "What's my obligation in this situation?" When you clarify your obligations and responsibilities, it's easier to enforce your boundaries. It may sound simple at first, but two great examples from my own life show otherwise: fundraisers and volunteering.

Remember the ASPCA commercials with all the sad puppy faces in cages while the song "Angel" by Sarah McLachlan played in the background? Yeah—I cried every single time those came on. I've been a volunteer with multiple different Humane Societies over the years. I walked dogs for them during college and while I lived in an apartment. I've adopted dogs from the Humane Society. At the time of this writing, I've been an executive board member for our local Humane Society going on six years. I've donated money and volunteered many hours for other charities and events throughout my life, but I've committed the most to animals.

I'm telling you this because I used to have so much guilt around saying no to people asking me to donate to their charity. There are so many worthy causes out there, and I wanted to support them all! If a cashier asked me to round up for charity, I would always say yes. I didn't want to sound like an uncaring, cold-hearted person! Unfortunately, I wasn't prepared to handle the question, so when it caught me by surprise, I defaulted to the impression I wanted to give a stranger—kindness.

You would not be in the wrong for making a donation to charity by rounding up at the cash register. It's spare change! But if you stop to think about ALL the different charities you contribute to, the donations add up. So, what are your charitable obligations? How do you say no to a charity outside of the ones you already contribute to?

What I've learned to say in response to those donation requests: "Not at this time; I already have charities I chose to support this year."

Clarifying your obligations and your means of enforcing your boundaries can help in many areas of your life, not just your personal safety.

If you are trying to figure out how understanding your obligation to help others ties to personal safety, think of the Ted Bundy example I used earlier. By manipulating his victims' kindness and a feeling of duty to help someone in need, he did not need to use physical force to lure them to his vehicle and their eventual death.

Obviously, those were examples with tragic outcomes. I can't give you the exact warning signs to look for concerning your personal safety because context matters. However, I can help you sharpen the foundational skills needed to build mental strategies for handling whatever comes your way by starting small. Clarifying your obligations in those small scenarios, such as rounding up at the cash register, will make focusing easier in general, including times when your personal safety is on the line.

Daily Habit: What's Your Obligation?

Throughout this chapter, you learned about the importance of deciding your obligation to others ahead of time. Setting these guidelines in your mind and getting comfortable with enforcing them prevents the manipulation of your kindness and co-dependent relationships in the future.

- ◆ If someone in your immediate family needed help, what are you willing to do and not willing to do?
- ◆ Decide which friends for whom you would be willing to get up in the middle of the night if they called you.
- ◆ Make a list of your current obligations. Cross out any non-critical ones that make you feel drained or that you dread taking part in.
- ◆ If a stranger asks you for help and you don't want to, what are other options you can give them?

Make sure to get on Instagram and share what new things you discovered about yourself with the hashtags #sharpwomen #daily-habits, and remember to tag @TheDiamondArrowGroup!

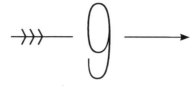

Turning the Tables

The most common way people give up their power
is by thinking they don't have any.

—Alice Walker

like to talk. A lot. Especially on the topic of situational awareness. I've had to work hard to change that about myself to make my personal safety a priority. It's safer to do less talking and more listening.

Meeting new people and learning their stories is one of my favorite things to do. If you're an introvert by nature, you might be cringing right now. However, even if you consider yourself an extrovert, you may still prefer deep discussions instead of superficial conversations. Either way, when interacting with someone you don't know, you need to be cautious about the personal information you give away.

Does awkward silence make you uncomfortable? Do you like to make small talk with the rideshare driver or the stranger next to you in line? Don't worry; I'm not going to say you can't be a friendly person. Instead, I'm going to help you sharpen your ability to be a fascinating person without saying a word.

Tell Me More about You

Ben sat down in the seat next to me on the airplane. I could tell he was going to be a talker by his friendly demeanor. Even though I had my book ready to start reading during the flight, I engaged in conversation. I discovered he had many interesting stories to share, and the two-hour flight time passed quickly. When we boarded the next plane after the layover, we sat next to each other to continue our chat. I shared a little bit about my passion for helping women (this was prior to starting The Diamond Arrow Group), and he offered to connect me with some influential women in his industry. We exchanged business cards and parted ways.

A year later, I discovered illegal business practices at the small company where I was employed. When I brought them to the attention of the owner, I was fired. Ben offered me a contract position with his company to help get my family and me back on our feet. I didn't have any experience in his industry, but I was comfortable meeting new people and building relationships. Stepping out of my comfort zone was scary, but I couldn't pass up the opportunity for professional growth. Whenever someone asked him how we had connected originally, he told them I was one of the most interesting people he had ever met on an airplane. While it was flattering, I had to laugh because, from my perspective, he had done most of the talking!

It feels good when someone is genuinely interested in learning about you. It's wonderful when you can tell they are listening by the questions they ask. Many therapists would be out of their jobs if individuals felt the people in their lives heard them! Communicating authentically is a skill you can use to improve many areas of your life beyond personal safety, including at home, at work, and with friends.

I want to explain how I differentiate between the phrases "**communicate authentically**" and "**communicate effectively**."

Someone with **effective communication** skills can get information out of you that you don't want to share. For example, parents will use these skills to determine who ate the last cookie out of the cookie jar. Have you ever been in a conversation with someone really good at getting you to tell them things you never intended to tell them? When Daria and Mitchell first started dating, he used his investigative skills as a cop to find her weakness. She brushed off his deeply personal questions at the early stages of getting to know each other as a sign of sincere interest. Unfortunately, Daria didn't think to turn the tables and question why he wanted to know such specific information.

He also used those effective communication skills to see how she would respond to certain questions and things he said. In his twisted mind, he liked Daria's headstrong and stubborn nature because it was a challenge. He thought he was superior to her and looked forward to breaking her spirit. But he underestimated her.

Sometimes it's not about getting information out of you; it's about impacting your emotions. When something triggers you, you may respond from an irrational or emotional state of mind. It's the metaphor of stirring the pot or poking the bear. It's the slight jab at your character which causes you to feel the need to defend yourself.

"Here, let me help you with that flat tire."

"No thanks, I've got it."

"Come on now, don't let your pride get in the way of accepting help!"

Declining his offer of assistance might not have had anything to do with your pride, but when he says that, you feel compelled to defend or explain your answer.

Don't. You said no. End of story.

Why Do You Want to Know?

When someone asks you a question you don't want to answer, you can ask, "Why do you want to know?" to discover their intentions. They may have no ill intent; they're possibly truly being curious. Turning the tables and asking them why they want to know also gives you time to decide if you want to answer. As mentioned in chapter 8, you are not obligated to respond to personal questions you don't want to answer, especially from people you've just met.

"Do you live around here?"

"Why do you ask?"

"Which building do you work in?"

"Oh, do you work around here?"

No Really, Judge a Book by Its Cover

Potential attackers ARE looking at what information you give away without saying a word. How much personal information are the stickers on your car, the clothing you wear, and the things in the backgrounds of your photos posted online telling people?

Evaluate your personal safety by looking at your life from an outsider's perspective. What could a stalker learn about your daily routine, your favorite places, and where you live and work without talking to you? Try this exercise on others and see how much information you can gather about their day-to-day activities. Turn the tables and pretend you're a private investigator. If that feels creepy to you, take it as a sign that your potential to be a stalker is low, at least lower than criminal levels.

Turn the Tables on Yourself

A private client of mine needed to review and limit her personal information available online. Because she and I were connected already, I reached out to a friend who is knowledgeable in this space and had zero connections with her. What he was able to find out shocked her.

He was able to identify every member of her family, where they worked, and where her kids went to school. He figured out their home address and favorite restaurants. He even found her husband's last marathon run time. While some of this may seem insignificant as individual pieces of information, when combined in a criminal mindset, the options for psychological threats from a stalker are limitless. It may not seem important to limit the information you share online. Maybe you're saying right now, "Who would want to stalk me?" Again: no one wakes up thinking they'll be a victim today. Situational awareness is prevention to avoid potential threats in the future. After you've become the target of a stalker, it's too late to take personal information off the internet.

Your Professional Life

You may not have a lot of control over the information shared as it relates to your career. Depending on your field, you may be required to wear a uniform with your name on it. In certain instances, such as at conferences or conventions when you're wearing a name badge on a lanyard, you may be unwittingly broadcasting the places you go and things you do for everyone to see.

I understand why a name badge is necessary during the event, but you need to take it off and put it in your purse or bag outside of the event activities. The badge gives your name and what event you're attending. Noting it, someone with a criminal mindset will easily deduce you're only in town for a short while and more than likely alone in your hotel room. If they take it to the next level, they can search for the conference agenda online and know when and where to find you. Get in the habit of removing your name badge every time you leave the event space.

'I Don't Get It'

I forget where I originally read this life hack, but it's brilliant, and I want to share it with as many women as possible.

If a guy makes an inappropriate joke that makes you uncomfortable, turn the tables on them. Adopt a puzzled look.

"I don't get it; what do you mean?"

This can effectively shut down any further comments because now they have to explain what they found funny about their offensive joke.

Daily Habit: Get Curious

A big part of building your situational awareness skills is simply about being curious. The great thing is that you don't need to focus only on spotting danger; you also want to get curious about what's normal in your environment. Once you start building what's called the baseline of your surroundings and the people in that baseline, it will be much easier to notice when there's an anomaly—something that shouldn't be there or something that's missing. You also want to get curious about the nonverbal signals people give off. Building these skills helps in reading strangers and noticing when a loved one has had a bad day.

* During your daily commute, try to spot one new landmark you've never noticed before.
* Pick a day this week to notice everyone's eye color.
* The next time you're sitting somewhere public and have spare time, observe people around you and guess what their mood is.
* Work on your interview skills! Practice keeping the conversation focused on the other person, especially people you've just met.

Make sure to get on Instagram and share the new things you discovered about your environment with the hashtags #sharpwomen and #dailyhabits—and remember to tag @TheDiamondArrowGroup!

Sharp Kids

Courage, sacrifice, determination, commitment,
toughness, heart, talent, guts. That's what little girls
are made of; the heck with sugar and spice.

—Bethany Hamilton

Use your manners, be polite, be kind, don't make others feel bad, help those in need, and look for the best in everyone. You heard these social mores while you were growing up. If you have kids, you've probably passed along these golden rules to them. As an adult, it's easy to assume your kids will understand how to apply these messages in their interactions with others.

When you say, "Don't make others feel bad," you are trying to prevent them from becoming the class bully.

However, the next lesson should be explaining when it's okay **not** to put others' feelings first. They need to recognize their own mental and physical boundaries and respectfully but firmly articulate those boundaries to others.

They Have a Superpower

How can you talk to kids about safety in a way that's age-appropriate? Get curious. I will offer some tips and ideas on what to teach kids, but ultimately, you know your kid(s) best. Ignoring the subject and hoping they never have a traumatic experience is not the answer. Their main personal safety issue isn't strangers; it's inappropriate behaviors.

The great thing about your kid(s) is their natural curiosity about the world. It's their superpower. It can also be a source of frustration when they won't stop asking you, "Why? Why? Why? Why? WHY??"

Staying curious about your environment is a foundational skill in increasing your situational awareness at any age. You can tap into your own natural superpower by seeing the world through your kid's eyes. Regain your childlike curiosity of the world with the added benefit of your life experiences filtering what you see. This is a great way to discover your own unconscious biases. When your kid asks you why and you give an answer, to which they ask again, "But, why?" Pause and think. *Was my answer actually true, or was it based on an assumption in my head?*

For example, say you're driving around running errands with your kid, playing a game of "spot the pedestrian" to build their observation skills. The stoplight ahead turns red. As you come to a stop, Fred asks from the back seat, "What does 'homeless' mean, Mommy?"

Caught off guard because you weren't expecting that question, you ask, "Why do you want to know, buddy?"

He points to a man standing on the sidewalk holding a cardboard sign asking for spare change.

How you answer your kid's question will tell you a lot about your unconscious biases around homelessness. For example, is your answer centered on your opinions of homeless individuals, or is it a simple definition?

That's how you can tap into the superpower of childlike curiosity to uncover the subconscious filter in which you view the world. Fred's question is about a word, not a person. Your opinion of homelessness is based on things such as interactions you've experienced with homeless individuals, things you've read and heard, or the opinions of influential people in your life. As a result, your explanation of "homeless" may differ from Merriam-Webster's definition, which is "having no home or permanent place of residence."[19]

If this example made you realize you have a bias and now you're feeling ashamed, don't! Instead, use it as an opportunity to sharpen your skills using your kid's natural curiosity to your advantage.

Let Them Lead

When your kids ask you a question you don't know how to answer, think back to chapter 9, and turn the tables. Answer their question with another question.

"What do you think it means?"

Let them lead the conversation to understand what exactly they are asking. This approach with kids, answering a question with a question, comes in handy with many topics. For example, when my oldest was around five years old, he asked me, "What's the difference between girls and boys?"

My brain panicked. *Is it time for these conversations already?!* To stall and give me some time to think, I turned the question around.

"What do you think is the difference?"

"Boys have short hair and stand when they pee. Girls have long hair and sit when they pee."

---

[19] "Homeless," Merriam-Webster Online, accessed October 27, 2021, https://www.merriam-webster.com/dictionary/homeless.

I laughed and felt a sense of relief. His perspective was based on the view of his small world. My husband is bald, and I have long hair. He wasn't looking for a full-blown conversation about the birds and the bees.

When kids ask questions, they are coming from their perspective, not yours. It's easy for you and me to forget that and respond as if we were speaking to another adult. This is your reminder to seek to understand the kids' perspective.

Age-Appropriate Conversations

More than likely, you were told as a child to "never talk to strangers." You've probably repeated this message to your kids. But the reality is, someday, your child is going to have to talk to a stranger. On my website, I offer the following advice:

Between the ages of four to six is a good time to start talking about strangers. This is the time most kids are starting school and interacting with many adults they don't know. A great question to start with is, "Do you know what a stranger is?" If they aren't sure, let them know a stranger is someone they don't know. Go through a list of people they know and then list people they don't know to help show them the difference. It's important not to scare them. Remind them that a stranger is not necessarily a good or bad person; a stranger is someone they don't know.[20]

It's easy for kids to wander off due to their natural curiosity at that age. When they realize you are no longer in their sights, they may panic, and if you haven't taught them what to do, they won't know how to make safe decisions. One suggestion is to pre-select a meeting spot at your destination (for instance, by the coffee shop

---

[20] Kelly Sayre, "Situational Awareness and Kids," The Diamond Arrow Group, June 9, 2019, https://thediamondarrowgroup.com/situational-awareness-kids/.

in the store or by the mini-donut concession stand) in case they get separated from you. Or tell them to find a woman. Yes—as mentioned before, tell them specifically to find a woman. Traditionally, women are caregivers, and whether or not they have kids, women are far more reliable in helping children through a situation to the end.[21] It's important to teach them which stranger to ask for help and how to ask for help.

Between the ages of seven to ten, have them practice talking to strangers while you are close by. Start with something simple. Have your child order their own food at a restaurant. Doing so builds their confidence and ability to interact with strangers. They need to know what they want in their heads and successfully articulate it to others. This exercise helps them realize it's their responsibility to get what they want/don't want through clear communication.

Between the ages of eleven to thirteen, children tend to be in activities beyond school. This is a great time to help them recognize and listen to their intuition signals while interacting with other adults such as coaches and volunteer leaders. Ask them how they felt during the conversation. Did they feel heard? Did the adult make eye contact and stay present while they were talking? Did any of the adult's actions or words make them uncomfortable?

"It felt uncomfortable when that person stood so close to me."

Your child needs to understand that their feelings matter. Articulating actions, behaviors, or what was said during a conversation is an important foundational skill in situational awareness. Don't dismiss or downplay their feelings and perspective. Kids need to feel like they can tell you anything.[22] They need to know you will listen to and believe them.

---

[21] Sayre, "Situational Awareness and Kids."

[22] Sayre, "Situational Awareness and Kids."

When kids reach high school, usually around the ages of fourteen to eighteen, they're going to experience all kinds of growth and change. They are going to test boundaries and push for independence. It's more important to be their parent than their friend. Set boundaries to protect them and show them how to set healthy boundaries for themselves. Talk to them. Ask about their friends, where they're going, and about their feelings. Teach them how to differentiate between behaviors and the person displaying the behavior. Remind them to stay curious about the other person's intentions.

Skill Building through Play

What's one of the biggest complaints of adults? Kids don't listen! In stores or crowded areas, kids want to explore. They aren't mature enough to be aware of a dangerous situation or person. They simply don't have enough life experience yet.[23] So when your instincts tell you something or someone is off, how can you get kids to pay attention and get closer to you immediately?

Come up with a safety word. Tell your kids that if they hear the safety word, they need to stop whatever they're doing and get close to you. Keep it simple. Avoid using a word commonly said in your home (such as "car," "doll," or "Legos") or a word that might be confusing. Depending on where you live, you could use words like "avalanche," "hurricane," or "iceberg."

The key to practicing their response to the safety word is to clearly say out loud beforehand, "This is for practice." You also don't want to test them too often, or the word will lose its effectiveness. Only share this safety word with the key adults in your child's life. You would never want someone to abuse this safety word to gain control of your child.

---

[23] Sayre, "Situational Awareness and Kids."

Using games to build their sensory skills makes sharpening their safety skills fun. Andy from *The Secure Dad Podcast* created a game for his young kids to look for exits in a building. He would ask them to count the doors. This was a non-threatening way to build their habit of looking for emergency exits everywhere they went.

Playing Marco Polo helps build the skill of locating people through hearing. When you're outside, ask them to describe what they can smell. After they get dressed in the morning, ask them what their clothes feel like on their skin. Have fun with it! Obviously, these games are easier to play with younger kids. Make modifications to the questions or games based on your kids' ages. Try and incorporate things they are interested in right now. You know your kids best!

A great game Jason from *The Safest Family on the Block* shared with me involves comparing the cars next to yours when you park. This builds articulation and description skills. It can also help you and your kids learn to recognize the make and models of cars. This skill can come in handy if you ever have to make a suspicious vehicle report.

Getting to Safety with Kids

While building your entire family's situational awareness skills, not only are you having fun, but you're also actually interacting more with each other. It's a win/win! The next step is deciding your family's plan in an active threat situation. What are you going to do if you need to get to safety quickly?

Let's say you're at the grocery store or some other large retailer with your kids, and you hear gunshots. What would you do? Here are a few key things to think about to get started.

Get Kids Safe Quickly

♦ Even if you've never heard a gunshot in person, don't second guess your intuition telling you it was.

♦ Stay calm. You need to **get to safety**, not just away from danger. Manage your adrenaline as much as possible to stay alert and aware of your surroundings.

♦ Use your safety word to get your kids next to you and ready to take direction from you.

♦ Consider the current mobility of your kids. Are you dealing with baby carriers, strollers, or kids buckled in shopping carts?

♦ Only take personal items that are absolutely necessary! This may mean leaving your cell phone behind. Don't weigh yourself down. You need to focus on getting yourself and your kids to safety immediately.

♦ Practice moving quickly with small children while keeping them from making noise that draws attention (this is a challenge).

Know the difference between cover and concealment in case you can't exit the building. Cover would stop or slow a bullet (a concrete wall, a heavy planter box), while concealment is a hiding spot but would not stop a bullet.

If your heart is beating a little faster right now, that's normal. Mentally going through how you would react in an active threat situation will affect you physically. The important thing to remember is your body can't go where your brain hasn't. Simply playing through a mental scenario in the safety of your home could make the difference between life or death in a real-world scenario.

Once you have your plan put together, share it with the rest of your family. Talk through the plan and make sure everyone understands it.

Daily Habit: Get Curious, Kids' Edition

If you're not sure how to start the safety and situational awareness conversation with kids, get curious. Talk with them and ask what they think about things. Teach them to pay attention to behaviors and let them know what is appropriate and what is not. Remember, their main personal safety issue isn't strangers; it's inappropriate human behaviors.

- Count the doors from *The Secure Dad* game to look for exits every time you enter a building.
- Compare the cars parked next to you as in *The Safest Family on The Block*. This works on kids' articulation and description skills.
- Play Marco Polo to work on their sense of hearing.
- Guess the mood. Ask your kids to figure out what type of mood someone is in by reading their body language.
- Play sensory games. What do they see, hear, smell, feel?
- Get them thinking. Which stranger would you ask for help?

Kids say the darndest things, and we'd love to hear about it! If you have funny stories from playing these games, make sure to share them on Instagram with the hashtags #sharpwomen #dailyhabits #kidsafety, and don't forget to tag @TheDiamondArrowGroup!

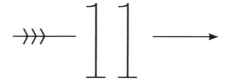

Vehicle Safety

A dame that knows the ropes isn't likely to get tied up.
—Mae West

've been a car aficionado for as long as I can remember. I wanted to sit and listen to my dad, uncles, and male cousins talk about engines and motors and horsepower. I have pictures of me lying on the ground watching Dad change the oil as a little girl. If Mom called me inside to help in the kitchen, I demanded to know why I couldn't stay in the garage like my brother.

Discussing anything related to vehicles is fun for me. It wasn't until I was out of high school that I realized not all women felt the same way. Why does any of this matter to you? Because you may not have expected a book on situational awareness for women to include an entire chapter on vehicle safety. I shared all of that to grease the wheels for this next chapter. (Get it? Ha!)

Lock Your Doors!

Katie and her daughter Layla were attending one of my mother-daughter classes. An incident had happened to her daughter and three friends at the local shopping mall, so they wanted to sharpen their personal safety skills.

Layla and her friends had arrived at the mall in two separate vehicles. When it was time to leave, they got into one car to decide what they wanted to do next. Suddenly, they heard a loud thud, and a man walked up to Layla's driver's window and motioned for her to roll down the window. Layla eyed him suspiciously and barely cracked the window.

"I'm so sorry, but I hit your car with my shopping cart. You should probably get out and take a look."

Layla's intuition alarm bells started going off.

"It's okay. It's an old car, and I'll have my parents take a look later."

"No, really, you should get out and look at the damage. I'm not going to hurt you!"

She hadn't initially thought he might hurt her, but after his last comment, she wasn't so sure. In the book *Gift of Fear*, de Becker says all unsolicited promises should be met with suspicion. [24]

Thankfully, Layla and her friends never got out of the car. They decided to leave the parking lot immediately and come back for the second car later. When Layla shared the story in class, she mentioned that her friends were pretty sure they saw the man get in a truck with another guy and start following them. But after a few traffic lights, they never saw them again.

Katie was so impressed with how her daughter had handled the situation. She admitted she would've probably gotten out of the car. As someone paying for car insurance and knowing her deductible,

---

[24] De Becker, *Gift of Fear*, 63.

she would have been pissed at the man! Everyone in the class laughed, and the other moms nodded their heads in agreement.

When the laughter subsided, I asked Layla if her car doors had been locked in that incident. She groaned and rolled her eyes, glanced at her mom, and then looked back at me.

"I always lock my doors because Mom reminds me every time I get in the car!"

"And aren't you glad I do because of that time in the McDonald's drive-through?" replied Katie.

On a separate occasion, Layla was in the drive-through line of a McDonald's. A man tried getting into the passenger side of her car. If Katie hadn't been so adamant with Layla about locking the car doors, she might have ended up in a bad situation. That specific drive-through lane was next to a busy road of oncoming traffic. A two-foot vertical drop to the sidewalk created a barrier preventing someone from escaping the drive-through lanes and driving away. There was a car in front of her and a car behind her. She couldn't drive to escape the man without causing major vehicle damage.

The simple habit of always locking her car doors had prevented two potentially bad situations.

Change the Settings

Most vehicles allow you to choose your automatic lock settings. You can find the instructions to change the settings in your vehicle's owner's manual. If you don't have a physical copy of the manual, you can do an online search with the year, make, and model of your vehicle and the words "owner's manual." Typically, manuals are in PDF format and available for download. If you use a key fob to lock/unlock your car doors, set your vehicle's settings so the first push of the button only unlocks the driver's door. If you need to unlock all the doors, you have to push the button twice.

Even if you've changed the auto-lock settings in your vehicle, there may still be a span of time between getting in your vehicle and driving before it auto-locks. (My vehicle doesn't auto-lock until I put it into drive.) Manually locking your vehicle as soon as you get in may not seem like an important habit to create, but it can make a big difference in your safety. Here's an experience I had in a grocery store parking lot.

I try to back into all parking spots so it's easier for me to leave quickly in an emergency. At the grocery store, that's not a viable option. I need to get our mountain of groceries loaded in the back of my vehicle. I increase my awareness in that situation by looking around between loading grocery bags.

On this particular grocery trip, I had just gotten back in my vehicle and closed my door. As I was hitting the lock button, a man walked from behind the vehicle next to me and towards my door. He started to ask me for money through my window. I said "no" while putting the keys in the ignition. I started my vehicle and backed out.

It takes practice with a safety habit to make it a subconscious action. You're going to have moments where you wonder if you're overreacting or being paranoid. Practice anyway. I want you to strive to make your personal safety a priority.

What's in Your Trunk?

Remember the story of Steve and the woman stranded on the side of the road with a flat tire? I want you to know how to change a flat tire yourself or at least know where the tire and tools are located in your vehicle. (Side note: it's a good idea to check for these items now in case they were removed or damaged.)

Here are other key items I recommend having in your vehicle in case of an emergency.

Vehicle Safety Kit Recommendations

- First Aid Kit
- Jumper Cables
- Fire Extinguisher
- Folding Shovel
- Distilled Water or Water Filter System & a few Non-perishable Food Items (be mindful of climate!)
- Caution Triangles
- Red Bandana
- Bungee Cords
- Zip Ties or Duct Tape
- Feminine Products
- Flashlight
- Small Blanket
- Ice Scraper
- Spare Clothing Items (hats, gloves, poncho, etc.)
- Diaper Wipes

If you don't have any of these items currently in your vehicle, try purchasing one or two at a time and build your supply. You will need to make modifications depending on the climate you live in, the size of the vehicle, and your lifestyle. For example, if you have a child in diapers, make sure to have extra diapers in the car. I keep diaper wipes in my car because they are handy for wiping hands and cleaning up small spills. If they dry out, all I have to do is add a little water, and they are good to go.

Basic Vehicle Maintenance

Keeping your vehicle maintained is similar to situational awareness. Your goal is to **avoid** finding yourself stuck on the side of the road with vehicle troubles. Follow the recommended schedule for oil changes, fluid checks, and tire rotations. Stop ignoring the warning light on your dashboard and get it checked out! I've been in vehicles where the driver put a piece of black tape over the warning light because they were sick of looking at it. This is like ignoring your intuition signals telling you something is off in your environment. Don't do it.

If you're saying right now, "But I hate going to the mechanic's shop! They make me feel stupid. I worry they are going to rip me off because I'm a woman who doesn't know a lot about cars."

I get it, AND I recognize that you are sharpening your skills to handle the behaviors of others that make you uncomfortable. To find a mechanic or dealership you can trust, ask your female friends for recommendations. Look for online reviews of those businesses posted by women, or look for women-owned businesses. According to a *Forbes* article from 2019, women control 70-80 percent of all consumer purchasing decisions.[25] If we start flexing that purchasing influence when it comes to mechanics' shops, the good ones will rise to the top.

Another basic rule to follow is keeping your fuel tank above a quarter-tank full. I admit I've had my low fuel indicator light turn on more than I care to think about. I have run out of gas once in my life, and while it was a humorous experience, I never want it to happen again. You do not want to find yourself in an emergency situation and realize you're almost out of gas. On the maintenance side of this conversation, when you run your fuel to empty, the

---

[25] Krystle M. Davis, "20 Facts and Figures to Know When Marketing to Women," *Forbes*, May 13, 2019, https://www.forbes.com/sites/forbescontentmarketing /2019/05/13/20-facts-and-figures-to-know-when-marketing-to-women/?sh =8ef89641297e.

crud that naturally accumulates at the bottom of your fuel tank gets sucked into the engine. Engine repairs are expensive. Take the time to keep your fuel tank full.

It Corners Like It's on Rails

Working on your defensive driving skills can help you avoid hazards by increasing your awareness and speed in decision-making. Plus, it's fun to learn.

According to SafeMotorist.com, "defensive driving" means driving in a strategic way that "enables motorists to address identified hazards in a predictable manner." This approach goes beyond awareness of "basic traffic laws and procedures."[26]

While safe driving helps protect you from accidents, you may be wondering what defensive driving has to do with general personal safety.

The answer is "a lot."

Jurek Grabowski, research director for the AAA Foundation for Traffic Safety, says the average driver spends the equivalent of seven 40-hour workweeks behind the wheel each year. "It's clear that traveling by car remains a central part of American's lives," he says.[27]

In that same article, it mentions that women are 24 percent more likely than men to have a passenger in the vehicle on any given trip."[28] When you take turns carpooling, attending sports activities, even running errands, kids are typically involved. Not only does sharpening your defensive driving skills matter for you, but it also matters in protecting your loved ones.

---

[26] "What is Defensive Driving?" SafeMotorist.com, American Safety Council, accessed October 27, 2021, https://www.safemotorist.com/articles/Defensive_Driving/.

[27] Andrew Gross, "Americans Spend an Average of 17,600 Minutes Driving Each Year," AAA, September 28, 2016, https://newsroom.aaa.com/2016/09/americans-spend-average-17600-minutes-driving-year/.

[28] Andrew Gross, "Americans Spend an Average of 17,600 Minutes Driving Each Year."

Beyond Driving

Remaining aware of your surroundings while you're sitting at a traffic light can help you avoid a potential carjacking (keeping your doors locked at all times helps in this situation, too!). Watching the taillights of cars a few vehicles ahead of you increases your ability to react to slowing traffic more quickly, which prevents fender benders. Working on your peripheral vision while driving will help you notice animals, people, and bouncing balls more quickly when they unexpectedly enter your lane of traffic. Improving your driving skills is a key part of sharpening your personal safety.

Before Exiting Your Vehicle

You've arrived at your destination safely and found a great parking spot. Before you unlock your doors and get out of your vehicle, unbuckle yourself. If you need to get out of your car quickly, you'll be ready to move. Pause a moment to make sure you have what you need and check all your mirrors for a person close to your vehicle. This is a great time to decide which self-defense tool is the best fit for where you're going.

The distance between your vehicle and your destination is the transition area. Attacks are more likely to occur in this area because people are not fully alert and present. Plus, if the destination is part of your daily routine (going to work, for instance), a predator or abuser knows you're likely to be there.

Make Your Vehicle a Mobile Fortress

I want you to start looking at your vehicle as more than a mode of transportation. It's protection for you and your loved ones. It's a survival tool with supplies to keep you safe, warm, hydrated, and nourished for a short period of time if you become stranded. In a situation where you need to evacuate your home on short notice, you will be glad it has the basic necessities to make leaving quickly less stressful.

Daily Habit: Become a Mobile Maven

If you've never considered yourself someone who loves to learn about cars, it's time to start. Here are simple habits to get you started.

- ◆ Change the auto-lock settings on your vehicle with your personal safety in mind.
- ◆ Figure out where your spare tire and tools are located.
- ◆ Learn where and how to check fluid levels.
- ◆ Learn how to check the air pressure in your tires.
- ◆ Take inventory of the basic survival items in your vehicle. Over time, purchase what you are missing.
- ◆ Search for defensive driving classes near you and get registered.
- ◆ Practice checking your mirrors before exiting your vehicle. Include kids by having them look around as well.
- ◆ Change up your regular driving routes. Find new ways to get from Point A to Point B.

BONUS GAME: The ability to tell if the same vehicle is following you is very important to your personal safety. Practice guessing the make and model of vehicles to start familiarizing yourself with body styles. Being able to identify vehicles and give an accurate description will help in reporting suspicious vehicles to law enforcement.

Did you discover something new about your vehicle? Did you find a great safety gadget you think other women would like? Share what you learned on Instagram with the hashtags #sharpwomen #dailyhabits #vehiclesafety, and make sure to tag @TheDiamond ArrowGroup!

12

Environment/Travel Safety

Adventure should be part of everyone's life. It is the whole difference between being fully alive and just existing.

—Holly Morris

One of my favorite things to do is travel. From road trips to overseas flights, you won't have to ask me twice to go on an adventure. You can read all you want about a destination, but the best way to learn about it is to experience it in person. Whether you choose to travel solo or with others, here are some tips to stay safe before, during, and after your trip.

Explore the World

I had the opportunity to travel to Barcelona, Spain, for work. While I would meet up with others after I arrived, I had to get to the destination by myself. I thought, "This is wonderful, and even though I don't know how to speak Spanish more than asking for the bathroom and ordering another beer, I'm sure I'll be fine!" I sat down to do what I always do before traveling to a foreign destination—research. I quickly discovered the two official languages of Barcelona are Castilian and Catalan, variations of Spanish.

I wanted to know what the taxi stand outside the airport looked like and where it was located. I didn't know if the signage inside the airport would have an English translation, and I wanted to keep from looking like an obvious tourist. When I searched for the street view of the airport's exterior, I discovered I could walk inside the airport virtually. It was fantastic! From the comfort of my own home, I could see what the walk from my arrival gate to baggage claim and then out to the taxi stand looked like. I noticed that the interior signage did have the English translation. I could take a mental snapshot of the visual of the taxi stand so I would easily recognize it after I retrieved my luggage.

The next thing I did was search the driving route from the airport to my hotel. I noted any landmarks that would help confirm my taxi driver was going in the right direction. I also searched for my hotel and viewed the location in street view so I'd visually recognize it and know I was getting dropped off at the right place. All of this research built my confidence in traveling safely without needing to rely on my cell phone when I arrived. If my cell service was spotty or not working, I wouldn't be left with hoping my taxi driver was a good human.

Before You Go

You've spent days and maybe even weeks searching for lodging options and things to do while visiting your destination. It's also good to research the social media sites for local law enforcement and public safety. "Like" and follow their accounts and look at recent posts for information on areas of town to avoid and the typical crimes that happen in each area. This knowledge will help you know what criminal behaviors to look for when observing your surroundings.

If traveling outside your home country, review any travel advisory warnings by doing a keyword search of your destination using an online search engine: for instance, "Barcelona, Spain, travel advisory."

In the United States, you will end up on the US Department of State website, and I highly recommend reading over the information posted. While you're on their site, enroll in STEP, the Smart Traveler Enrollment Program. This free service allows US citizens and nationals traveling and living abroad to register their trips with the nearest US embassy or consulate. By doing this, you will receive important information from the embassy about safety conditions. The embassy can contact you for emergencies while you're in the country and help family and friends reach you regarding emergencies back home.[29]

When traveling alone, make sure someone else knows your travel plans and itinerary. If someone will meet you when you arrive, have their contact information, and set a pre-determined location to meet. Then, if you have communication troubles after you arrive, you'll already have a mutually understood meeting point. You should review your cell-phone coverage options before traveling overseas and have a backup plan in case it's not as advertised.

Scan your credit cards, driver's license, and passport into a document. Save a copy to the cloud, or leave it with someone back home who can email it to you quickly and easily. That way, if those documents get lost or stolen, you can access the information anywhere with an internet connection.

What to Pack

It's important to bring the right clothing and shoes on your trip. You want to be comfortable and culturally appropriate for your

---

[29] "Smart Traveler Enrollment Program," US Department of State, accessed October 29, 2021, https://step.state.gov/STEP/Index.aspx.

destination. One life hack I use when figuring out what clothing to pack is searching online for live webcams. Here is an example: "Barcelona, Spain, live webcam."

Many top destinations have live camera feeds, which I like to check to see what people are wearing. It's similar to the "gray man" intention of blending in with the public. You want to lower your risk of looking like a tourist by dressing similar to the locals. When possible, leave high-value items such as expensive jewelry at home.

Leave at home any clothing items that identify where you are from, where you work, or what school you attend. I get it; you want to show pride in those things, but doing so does not prioritize your personal safety. Take your work logo wear as an example. It's easy for someone with a criminal mindset to search your company's website for your photo. If your picture appears in the "About Us" section, now they have your name, your title, and a good idea of where you live. A con artist would be able to use that information to act like they know you and try and gain your trust. Don't make it easy by helping them know where to start looking for clues.

During Your Trip

Take lots of pictures! Every cab or rideshare you get into, take a picture of the driver's ID sign posted in the back seat. Also, photograph the cross-street sign near your lodging in case you get lost as you're out walking around. That information gives you a safe way to ask for help finding your hotel in a larger city without overtly giving away where you're staying.

If you don't like pictures of yourself, you're not going to like my next recommendation. Take selfies with the new people you meet. Most people have their phones automatically back up to the cloud. Taking pictures provides a visual record of your activities to look back on with automatic date, time, and location information saved in the metadata. If something should happen to you, friends or family can access your cloud and see pictures of the people you were with and the places you visited. It will establish a timeline with locations for authorities to know where to start looking for you.

If you're staying at a hotel, make sure to leave the key card sleeve in your room. You don't want to advertise where you are staying and your room number when you're out in public. When possible, request a room on the second to sixth floors at check-in. You don't want to be on the ground floor for safety reasons, and the sixth floor is the max reach for most fire department ladder trucks. In case of a fire, you'll be able to exit through a window.

Before staying at a vacation home rental, research all reviews on the owners or property managers. If anything seems suspicious or unsafe, don't make a reservation. Do an online street view of the address to see what the surrounding area looks like. Photos used to advertise a place are taken at the right time of day and with flattering angles to create an optimal vision in your head. By using the street view search option, you will get a more realistic picture. That being said, keep in mind the date the street view image was captured. I've rented an Airbnb that had been purchased in foreclosure and renovated. The street view of that place was prior to the renovation and not flattering!

While Exploring

When you're out exploring your destination, be careful of what information you share. Don't share how long you're in town, where you're staying and whether or not you're staying alone. Do NOT open your door to unsolicited hotel staff. Stay in a relaxed, alert state of mind. Keep your head up, look around and observe your surroundings. Refrain from wearing earbuds when you're exploring the area and choose well-lit and populated routes while walking. Hang the Do Not Disturb sign and lock the deadbolt when you're in your room. Most of all, trust your gut. If something doesn't feel right, it probably isn't.

Before you leave your place of lodging, be mindful of what you throw away in the garbage. Keep any papers containing your personal information with you to throw away at home.

After Your Trip

When you get home, watch your bank and credit card accounts for any unauthorized spending in case your cards are compromised. This is also the time to share the pictures from your adventures on social platforms. It's not a good idea to share photos online while on vacation as it broadcasts that you are not home.

The world is a big, wonderful place filled with lots of interesting people. I want you to feel confident traveling to see friends, family, and all those places on your bucket list. Taking the time to properly prepare before your next trip will help you feel confident in your ability to stay safe while exploring new places.

Daily Habit: Do Your Research

The more you research before you travel, the less stressed you'll be, as well as more prepared to handle an emergency.

- Search online for any travel advisory warnings regarding your destination.
- View live webcams of the destination to see what type of clothing locals wear so you can pack accordingly.
- Use the street view function of online maps at points of interest of your destination.
- Create contingency plans in case your original plans change at any point during your travels.

What is one travel safety tip you learned in this chapter? What other safety measures do you put in place to ensure a relaxing and enjoyable trip? Share your thoughts via Instagram with the hashtags #sharpwomen #dailyhabits #travelsafety, and make sure to tag @TheDiamondArrowGroup!

This Is Only the Beginning

*Self-care isn't always oils and baths. Sometimes it is seeing
who you are and giving yourself permission to be. It is
setting boundaries and saying no. Self-love is knowing
your worth and not having guilt about doing you.*

—Simi Fromen

Why I Wrote This Book

I wrote this book because it was something that even a crazy pandemic and the outside world couldn't stop me from doing. I saw the increase of violence against women and children as they were trapped with their abusers during lockdowns, and I knew this information needed to get out of my head and down on paper.

What I didn't expect from writing this book was gaining clarity about events in *my* past. My journey of studying situational awareness has helped me see my life experiences from a different perspective. Where I once felt immense shame and guilt, I could finally forgive myself for not having the knowledge, words, and tools to see situations for what they really were. In some of those experiences, I trusted my intuition and went against what everyone around me was telling me to do. The aftermath of trusting my gut and doing what was best for me had great negative consequences in certain aspects of my life. Family and so-called friends disowned me. People labeled me as something I wasn't. I chose to leave everything behind and move thousands of miles away with a friend to feel like I could breathe again. Though I learned so much about myself through all of that, I'm stubborn, and I did not learn the important lesson of trusting my intuition. That required many more face-plants and mistakes of looking to others for advice on living my life.

And guess what? I'm still learning. I'm still sharpening my skills every day: mentally, physically, and emotionally. If 80-90 percent of attacks on women come from someone they know, then the early warning signs of controlling and abusive behaviors need to be part of the self-defense conversation. The attacks you face will start with subtle tests of your boundaries. As it is in nature, predators watch their prey. They make small movements to remain undetected as they get closer to their target. If the prey is alert and becomes aware of being hunted, it will act to get away from the danger. It doesn't sit around to wait and see if it's a "friendly" predator, just playing games.

With its original target gone, the predator looks for the next prey. The cycle of testing the new target's awareness starts all over again.

It's easier for instructors to teach from the "stranger danger" mindset because it doesn't involve relationship status, emotional responses, social mores, and financial implications. It's easier to think of the predator as a scary stranger lurking in the dark. You can have a false sense of security because you don't live in a bad neighborhood, you don't walk down dark streets late at night, and you avoid anyone who "looks scary." It won't happen to you because you carry a fill-in-the-blank tool for self-defense. Unfortunately, if you're only focused on stranger danger, you will miss the early warning signs of threatening behaviors coming from someone you live with or see every day—even the "hometown hero."

Physical Defense

Can you picture yourself causing physical damage to a scary-looking predator, jumping out from behind the bushes? What about causing damage to someone you know who "let his anger get the best of him" and swears it'll never happen again?

What about your wonderful grandmother, who is in her last chapter of life and has a tendency to physically lash out? Are you going to block with your left and punch her with your right?

How about your young child on the spectrum? They have the potential to seriously injure themselves and others when they're in crisis. It's important to know how to control their movements without causing them harm. Detecting the early warning signs of an oncoming crisis and de-escalating it beforehand is better for everyone.

What about the boss who starts rubbing the back of your neck while sitting next to you? Are you going to throw an elbow to his face and break his nose?

These and so many other unique situations are the threats to your safety that you actually face every day. But no one has talked to you about them in a way that takes your perspective into consideration. Yes, there are self-defense instructors out there talking about the real ways women experience violence. Yet how many of those instructors are women? This is not discounting the knowledge and training of male instructors; it's simply stating a fact. Men joke about not understanding how women think. How can they begin to understand our perspective on the threatening behaviors we face? They can't. They don't know what it's like to be a woman.

Start Your Journey

Learning to become more situationally aware is a journey. There is not one perfect path to follow. There is not one perfect tempo in which to learn. There isn't even perfect 24/7 situational awareness! You get to pick how you want to practice the daily habits I gave you at the end of each chapter. Work on practicing one habit until you feel comfortable doing it. Then, either layer another daily habit on top of it or work on it separately. Remember, these are life skills you *already have*—you're just applying them to your personal safety now.

You will start seeing your world a little differently, noticing things you've never noticed before. You will be more present in your daily interactions with people, and your communications skills will improve. You will start to recognize your intuition signals faster and be able to act accordingly. The more you practice these habits, the more they will become part of your subconscious. Eventually, you won't even notice yourself doing them. You will walk with more confidence, and other people will notice.

If you just read that last paragraph from a personal safety perspective, go back and re-read it thinking about your career, your family, and your friends. That is what building true foundational skills to improve your life looks like. You will use the information this book provides to make the most of these skills in multiple areas.

This is why it's important to be realistic about what you feel comfortable and confident doing and mentally planning with those things in mind. These elements make all the difference when it comes to your personal safety. My goal is to create a space where you feel safe enough to ask every question on your mind: a space where you enjoy learning about self-defense and how to improve your situational awareness skills. It can be extremely uncomfortable to think about being attacked. It can be absolutely heartbreaking to realize you are in an abusive relationship. It can be overwhelming to think about regaining your confidence to live life after an attack.

I know you can do it. You are a Sharp Woman.

You grew up in a world that places a lot of outside expectations on you from the day you are born. You try to figure out who you are at your core while people around you second-guess your decisions. You handle all life's curveballs while still thinking of your loved one's needs before your own. That takes inner grit that only a Recon Marine could understand and appreciate. Maybe.

Let this book be the first step in building self-confidence in your personal safety skills. Ask lots of questions. Figure out what works best for you. Let's make it commonplace for women to take regular self-defense classes. Think of it as a new type of spin class. If that's a stretch, then start monthly. When you take action to sharpen your skills, other people will notice. Little girls will start to see that prioritizing personal safety is a normal thing to do. That they have worth and can own their space. That they don't have to ask anyone for permission to live life on their own terms.

You've got this.

Daily Habit: Mental Recall

The ability to accurately recall things you've seen and people you've met is key to your personal safety. Here's how to recognize if someone keeps showing up in the same places as you, as in Ann's story from the mall.

- Pick one thing to notice with everyone you meet. Pick something that is not easily changeable, such as their teeth when they smile (or if they don't show their teeth).
- At the end of the day, mentally play back as much as you can remember. How many details can you recall?

- What clothes are your kids/partner/roommates wearing today?
- The next time you leave a meeting, recall who was in attendance and what they were wearing.
- Start a journal. Include as many descriptive details as possible when writing about your day.

What's the one thing you're going to notice on everyone you meet? Share your thoughts via Instagram with the hashtags #sharpwomen #dailyhabits, and make sure to tag @TheDiamond ArrowGroup!

Sharp Women Unite

have one more person to thank, and it's you. Thank you for buying this book. Time is precious, so every moment you spend reading my book, writing a review, sending me an email with your comments, and sharing it with friends is a gift. I appreciate you.

This book is my rallying cry and jumping-off point. Help spread this information to all the women you care about so we can make a difference in the next generations of Sharp Women!

Be the Sharp Woman you were always meant to be.

Make sure to share your daily habit posts on social media and tag The Diamond Arrow Group so I can cheer you on!

✉ kelly@thediamondarrowgroup.com

◎ @TheDiamondArrowGroup

f @TheDiamondArrowGroup

in Kelly Sayre

⊕ www.thediamondarrowgroup.com

About the Author

KELLY SAYRE empowers women with realistic tactics and tools to help them live life safely and on their own terms. Her refreshing angle on women's safety emphasizes non-physical, proactive situational awareness techniques that recognize and avoid threatening situations *before* they happen.

With a grounded approach and high energy, Kelly works with law enforcement, nonprofit, corporate, and youth organizations on emergency preparedness, situational awareness training, and personal safety. She is a frequent speaker at national events and a guest on global podcasts.

Kelly is trained in FEMA's Community Emergency Response Team program, the Department of Homeland Security's Active Shooter Preparedness Workshop, and Texas A&M Extension Service's crisis communications. She is a licensed instructor for Prevention & Awareness at 500rising and a member of the Association of Threat Assessment Professionals, TeamWomen, and the Tri-County Humane Society. Kelly lives in Minnesota with her husband, children, and a 180-pound Great Dane.

Made in the USA
Monee, IL
12 April 2022